C000186844

Opening up
Galatians

DAVID CAMPBELL

DayOne

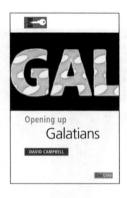

Galatians is a passionate, combative part of Scripture, one that is strikingly contemporary because it deals with a heresy which, in one form or another, is always with us. Salvation by ritual or character is a modern form of the 1st-century denial of the gospel which Paul confronts and demolishes. David Campbell opens up this letter in a most attractive and helpful way. His exposition is clear and the applications both challenging and encouraging. He deals with 'new perspectives' on Paul, not by analysing their errors but by stating and defending the truth which they call into question. This is pastoral wisdom. A timely and useful book.

Edward Donnelly, Minister, Trinity Reformed Presbyterian Church, Newtownabbey, Northern Ireland

Opening up Galatians by Pastor David Campbell is a delight to read. His engaging style is simple to follow and easy to understand. It is an excellent introductory commentary for God's people and a good model of simple explanation for the pastor. While clarifying the theology and message of the epistle, Pastor Campbell vividly introduces us to the actual people involved. The Judaizers, the Galatians themselves, and the apostle Paul come alive as living, breathing people. The interplay of their different thoughts and positions is not dealt with in an abstract manner but by drawing out the real-life implications of how a person lives before God.

A final recommendation concerns the well-thought-out questions in each chapter regarding the theological and practical implications of Paul's letter. These questions are good for Bible study

classes or just to stimulate the pastor in
what things to consider when preaching
the passage.

Overall, I highly commend Pastor
Campbell's little commentary for pastors
and people. It is much needed today, as
it was in Paul's day, to clarify the great
truth: justification by faith alone in
Christ alone.

**Dr Fred Malone, Pastor, First Baptist Church, Clinton,
Louisiana, USA**

To my fellow elders, with deep appreciation for their prayerful support throughout the writing of this book.

First printed 2010

ISBN 978-1-84625-190-0

British Library Cataloguing in Publication Data available
Published by Day One Publications
Ryelands Road, Leominster, England, HR6 8NZ
Telephone 01568 613 740   FAX 01568 611 473
email—sales@dayone.co.uk
web site—www.dayone.co.uk
North American e-mail—usasales@dayone.co.uk
North American web site—www.dayonebookstore.com

Printed by Gutenberg Press, Malta

Acknowledgements

I am deeply grateful to my friends and fellow ministers, Ted Donnelly and Fred Malone, for having taken the time to read through the manuscript, for their helpful comments, and for their warm commendations. Thanks are also due to my wife, Mairi, for her always valuable observations, and to my daughter, Megan, my in-house grammarian, who patiently puts her father's commas in the right places, and who in sundry other ways endeavours to improve his literary style.

List of Bible abbreviations

THE OLD TESTAMENT		1 Chr.	1 Chronicles	Dan.	Daniel
		2 Chr.	2 Chronicles	Hosea	Hosea
Gen.	Genesis	Ezra	Ezra	Joel	Joel
Exod.	Exodus	Neh.	Nehemiah	Amos	Amos
Lev.	Leviticus	Esth.	Esther	Obad.	Obadiah
Num.	Numbers	Job	Job	Jonah	Jonah
Deut.	Deuteronomy	Ps.	Psalms	Micah	Micah
Josh.	Joshua	Prov.	Proverbs	Nahum	Nahum
Judg.	Judges	Eccles.	Ecclesiastes	Hab.	Habakkuk
Ruth	Ruth	S.of S.	Song of Solomon	Zeph.	Zephaniah
1 Sam.	1 Samuel	Isa.	Isaiah	Hag.	Haggai
2 Sam.	2 Samuel	Jer.	Jeremiah	Zech.	Zechariah
1 Kings	1 Kings	Lam.	Lamentations	Mal.	Malachi
2 Kings	2 Kings	Ezek.	Ezekiel		

THE NEW TESTAMENT		Gal.	Galatians	Heb.	Hebrews
		Eph.	Ephesians	James	James
Matt.	Matthew	Phil.	Philippians	1 Peter	1 Peter
Mark	Mark	Col.	Colossians	2 Peter	2 Peter
Luke	Luke	1 Thes.	1 Thessalonians	1 John	1 John
John	John	2 Thes.	2 Thessalonians	2 John	2 John
Acts	Acts	1 Tim.	1 Timothy	3 John	3 John
Rom.	Romans	2 Tim.	2 Timothy	Jude	Jude
1 Cor.	1 Corinthians	Titus	Titus	Rev.	Revelation
2 Cor.	2 Corinthians	Philem.	Philemon		

Contents

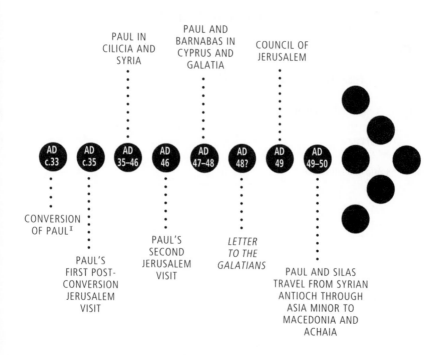

BLACK SEA

PISIDIAN ANTIOCH

ICONIUM

LYSTRA DERBE

SYRIAN ANTIOCH

CYPRUS

MEDITERRANEAN SEA

JERUSALEM

PAUL IN CILICIA AND SYRIA

PAUL AND BARNABAS IN CYPRUS AND GALATIA

COUNCIL OF JERUSALEM

AD c.33 | AD c.35 | AD 35–46 | AD 46 | AD 47–48 | AD 48? | AD 49 | AD 49–50

CONVERSION OF PAUL¹

PAUL'S FIRST POST-CONVERSION JERUSALEM VISIT

PAUL'S SECOND JERUSALEM VISIT

LETTER TO THE GALATIANS

PAUL AND SILAS TRAVEL FROM SYRIAN ANTIOCH THROUGH ASIA MINOR TO MACEDONIA AND ACHAIA

OPENING UP GALATIANS

Overview

Among the great evils that God overrules for good are the activities of those who teach false doctrine. In his inscrutable sovereignty God permits their false teaching to make inroads into the church, to spread far and wide, and often to do very considerable harm. At the same time, he is always in complete control of the situation and demonstrates that by overruling the false teaching for good.

We see it, for example, in the way in which the controversies generated by false teaching have led to a greater understanding of the truth. 'It holds almost universally in the history of the church', writes William Cunningham, 'that until a doctrine has been fully discussed in a controversial way by men of talent and learning taking opposite sides, men's opinions regarding it are generally obscure and indefinite and their language vague and confused, if not contradictory.'[2] Controversy has forced men to think with greater clarity. It has compelled them to examine the Scriptures more carefully and formulate their teaching more precisely than before. The result has been a greater understanding of the truth than previously existed, and a literature embodying that understanding that benefits future generations.

When we go back to the days of the apostles we see something even more basic: the activities of false teachers being overruled to the production of some of our foundational New Testament documents. It is striking to note just how much of the New Testament was written in response to false teaching. Paul's letter to the Colossians, his first letter to Timothy, his letter to Titus, his second letter to the Corinthians, John's letters, Peter's second letter, Jude—all to some extent were forged in the fires of controversy. So also was the letter to the Galatians. Galatians, indeed, is arguably the prime example.

It has to be said that aspects of the false doctrine attacked in this letter are no longer being taught in our churches. But Galatians is anything but outdated. The heresy it combats is, in its essence, widespread, and because of that the letter is no less necessary now than it was 2,000 years ago. Like the letter to the Romans, it gives us a very clear answer to that most vital of questions: How, as sinners, can we come to be right with the God against whom we have sinned? Nor does it leave it off before it has answered the related and no less important question: How, having become right with God, are we to progress in our Christian lives?

Background and summary

Opinions differ on the question of who the Galatians were, and interested readers will find the options discussed in scholarly commentaries.[1] My own preference is for the view that identifies them with the believers of Pisidian Antioch, Lystra, Derbe, and Iconium, cities that lay in the southern part of what the Romans, for decades, had been calling the province of Galatia. In Acts 13–14 Luke tells us the dramatic story of how, under the preaching of Paul and Barnabas, churches were established in these cities. There is considerable likelihood that these Galatian churches were the 'churches in Galatia' to whom Paul's letter was addressed (Gal. 1:2).

Of greater importance than the location of the churches is the grave situation they were facing and which occasioned the apostle's letter. At this point I will do no more than briefly summarize using the words of the letter itself. After greeting the Galatians, Paul says to them, 'I am astonished that you are so quickly deserting the one who called you by the grace of Christ and are turning to a different gospel—which is really no gospel at all. Evidently some people are throwing you into confusion and are trying to pervert the gospel of Christ' (1:6–7). Later, in the course of the commentary, we will be considering just who these troublers may have been, what their message was, how negatively they were impacting the believers, how the apostle sought to counteract their influence, and what it all has to say to the church today (which is a very great deal indeed!).

There are parts of Galatians that are difficult to understand, and it needs to be said up front that in this commentary a number of these difficulties are simply ignored. As someone who uses commentaries all the time, I appreciate how frustrating that may be for some readers and apologize in advance. It was simply not possible in a commentary of this size to tackle all the interpretive questions that a thinking reader might ask, even if the author had the competence to do so (which he does not). My hope is, however, that *Opening up Galatians* will form a helpful introduction to the letter and give the reader a sense of what it is basically about and what God is saying to us through it today. Some suggestions for further reading are given at the end of the book for those who wish to explore more fully Galatians' depths and riches.

One further matter. The traditional interpretation of Galatians has been challenged in recent years by advocates of the 'New Perspectives' on Paul. No attempt has been made in the commentary to engage with these New Perspectives. I have simply endeavoured to explain and defend the traditional Reformation understanding of this letter—particularly as regards the cardinal doctrine of justification by faith apart from the works of the law. For readers who are interested in a critique of the New Perspectives or who simply desire to study the doctrine of justification in depth, some books are listed at the end that will hopefully be helpful.

1 There's only the one gospel!

(1:1–10)

One of the great novels of the nineteenth century is Charles Dickens' *A Tale of Two Cities*. The letter to the Galatians could be given a similar title: *A Tale of Two Gospels*. Paul's 'tale', however, is factual, not fictional, and warns us that of the two gospels being heard in Galatia (and still being heard today), only one is true.

The first few verses of Galatians follow a pattern familiar to readers of the New Testament. The author tells us who he is ('Paul, an apostle'), identifies the ones to whom he is writing ('the churches in Galatia'), and pronounces a distinctively Christian blessing on them ('Grace and peace to you from God our Father and the Lord Jesus Christ').

It is good to linger over the introductions to New Testament letters because they are always rich in instruction. One noteworthy feature of the Galatians introduction, for instance, is the way in which the various elements of it are linked with both Jesus and the Father. Between these two persons of the Godhead there is absolute oneness of heart, mind, and purpose. They think, act, govern, and save *together* as they bring to fulfilment their joint eternal purpose. Three times this truth receives illustration in the introduction to Galatians. The Father and the Son are clearly at the heart of what is being said here, and very much 'hand in hand' in all that is going on. Their joint activities will serve as a useful framework for our study of these opening verses.

Together appointing Paul (vv. 1–2)

The letter begins with an emphatic denial: 'Paul, an apostle—sent not from men nor by man, but by Jesus Christ and God the Father, who raised him from the dead.' Human beings had nothing to do with the fact that Paul was an apostle—neither as source or as agent.

His apostleship, he says, was 'not from *men*'. No group such as the Twelve or the elders of one of the churches had made Paul an apostle. Nor was his apostolic position *by* man or *through* man. No one had been involved in conveying the divine will to him or mediating the divine appointment. The appointing was exclusively the act of Jesus and God the Father.

At one level this is just a standard opening note. The divine origin of his apostleship is something on which Paul touches frequently at the beginning of his letters. In Galatians, however, he is unusually emphatic on the point. Why so? The most likely reason lies in the activity and influence of certain men who were troubling the Galatian churches by preaching a seriously distorted gospel. It would seem that, in order to gain acceptance for their message, these men were attacking Paul's credentials as an apostle. *His* version of the gospel was not to be trusted, they were saying, because he was not the God-appointed apostle the Galatians had supposed him to be.

But he *was*, and it was that that gave him the right to be heard both then and now—and not just in regard to the gospel. In 1992 in Sydney, Australia, a supporter of women's ordination was reminded that the apostle Paul *opposed* their ordination. This was the man's reply: 'So what?'[1] It was of no importance to him what *Paul* taught. In reality, though, it is *all*-important, because as a divinely commissioned apostle Paul spoke with the authority of the God who sent him. That is why he could say to the Corinthians, for example, 'what I am writing to you is the Lord's command' (1 Cor. 14:37). That is why his witness to Christ—along with that of the other apostles—constitutes the foundation upon which the church is built (Eph. 2:20). By listening to Paul, we are listening to God himself. It is with that conviction that we approach his letter to the Galatians.

Together conveying blessing (v. 3)

As he often does in his introductions, Paul here invokes a blessing on his readers: 'Grace and peace to you from God our Father and the Lord Jesus Christ' (v. 3).

Grace has been beautifully defined as 'that goodwill on God's part which not only provides and applies salvation but blesses, cheers, and assists believers … that many-sided favour that comes in the form of hope to saints in despondency, of joy to them in sorrow, of patience to them in suffering, of victory to them under assault, and of final triumph to them in the hour of death'.[2] It is wonderfully comprehensive! Little wonder that Paul's prayerful wish for his beloved Galatians should be *grace*! It was just what they needed—and what we need as well.

> We look for grace and peace to the God who has made us his children and to the Christ who gave his life for us. Surely we will not look in vain!

So, too, the *peace* that he invokes. Peace in the midst of trials, peace that arises from a sense that we are right with God, peace that comes from trusting that all things are working together for our good, peace that keeps anxiety at bay—we all need constant supplies of it!

And what an encouragement to seek such blessings when we see from whom they are said to come: 'from God our Father and the Lord Jesus Christ, who gave himself for our sins'. We look for grace and peace to the God who has made us his children and to the Christ who gave his life for us. Surely we will not look in vain!

Together authoring salvation (vv. 4–5)

Verse 4 is a reference to the cross. There Jesus 'gave himself for our sins to rescue us from the present evil age'. And he did so 'according to the will of our God and Father'. The death of Jesus was at one and the same time a voluntary act of self-giving for the salvation of his people *and* an act of obedience to his Father in heaven. They were *together* in this!

The fruit of it for believers is deliverance from what is

described here as 'the present evil age'—the godless world to which all of us, on account of our fallenness, so naturally and tragically belong. Because of Calvary, the sin and the evil powers that shape the lives of so many of our fellow human beings (and once shaped ours) no longer control us. We have come instead under new, healthful, transforming influences which are changing us into the likeness of God and enabling us to live for him.

A 'different' gospel (vv. 6–10)

In most of Paul's letters his introductory greeting is followed either by thanksgiving to God for some aspect of his work in the lives of the believers to whom he is writing, or by praise to God. In this letter Paul got straight down to the main business. The situation created by the 'different' gospel (v. 6) to which the Galatians were being exposed was so alarming and such a burden on the apostle's spirit that he felt compelled to address it immediately.

The apostle Paul had been given the task by Jesus of 'testifying to the gospel of God's grace' (Acts 20:24), and it was *that* gospel he had preached in Galatia. In totally unmerited kindness God had sent his Son to live and die for sinners and now promised that, if they would but come to him in their need, they would in grace be forgiven and be granted eternal life. No need to try to earn salvation! No good works required in order to secure it! A simple reliance upon the Saviour—that's what Paul had proclaimed to the Galatians, and it was to that that they had responded in faith.

Then there came to Galatia a *second* gospel, 'a different gospel'. And it certainly was different. It admittedly had elements in common with the first, for it spoke of God's goodness to sinners in the gift of his Son and directed them to believe in him. But it insisted that something additional to faith was required. Simple reliance upon the Saviour (which had been Paul's message) was not enough. It was necessary to be circumcised as well and to obey the Law of Moses (we glean this both from the letter to the Galatians and from Acts 15). A right relationship with God could be enjoyed on no lesser terms.

The strains of this 'different' gospel are still being heard today. The details may have altered, but at heart it is just the same. Faith in Christ, though necessary, is not sufficient. Obedience to God's law, submission to the sacrament of baptism, a life characterized by good works, membership of a particular church, diligent efforts to get into and to keep oneself in God's good graces—these kinds of things are held to be just as important for salvation as faith in Jesus.

The apostle's verdict on this 'different' gospel

Paul's letter to the Galatians is a powerful repudiation of this different gospel and in these verses he gives us his opening salvo. The ESV captures well what Paul is saying as he moves from verse 6 to verse 7: the Galatians are 'turning to a different gospel—*not that there is another one*' (emphasis added). There is only the *one* gospel, the one message of salvation from God—not two. It is in that light that Paul gives his judgement: this 'different' gospel is not *another* gospel in the sense of being a valid alternative; it is nothing but a perversion (v. 7) of the divine original.

Our own verdict on its modern editions is to be the same.

Does the gospel that we are hearing give an exclusive place to grace? Does it send us to God with empty hands that we might receive salvation as a gift? Does it say to us that Christ by his life and death has done it all and that God requires nothing of *us*? Does it forbid us to try to supplement with our own works the perfectly sufficient work of Christ? If it does not, if it insists that, as well as believing in Christ, we must work to obtain God's favour by things such as submission to ceremonies, obedience to his law, and doing good, then what we are hearing is in fact 'no gospel at all' (v. 7) but rather a perversion of the gospel.

The tragic impact of this 'different' gospel

The opening note of this new section is an expression of astonishment that the Galatians were 'so quickly deserting the one who called [them] by the grace of Christ' and turning to this 'different' gospel (v. 6). Evidently, its preachers were enjoying alarming success. Not only were they getting a hearing, they were also getting a following. The Galatian believers were embracing this new message and as a consequence were beginning to observe the Law of Moses. At 4:10, for example, Paul says, 'You are observing special days and months and seasons and years!', while at 5:4 he addresses those who are 'trying to be justified by law'. There had been none of that when *he* had been there. He had preached that sinners were 'justified by faith in Christ and not by observing the law' (2:16), and the Galatians had accepted that as true. Not any longer.

Paul's language in verse 6 underscores the seriousness of what they were doing: 'you are ... deserting the one who called you by the grace of Christ'—namely, God himself. John Stott discloses some interesting facts about the word translated 'deserting': 'It signifies to "transfer one's allegiance". It is used of soldiers in the army who revolt or desert, and of men who change sides in politics or philosophy ... It is of this that Paul accuses the Galatians. They are religious turncoats, spiritual deserters.'[3]

Notice that it was not just a *message* they were deserting. To turn from the gospel of God's grace and attempt to be justified by law was to desert the very God who had so graciously called them. And Paul was simply astonished that they would do such a thing—and so quickly, too. How foolish they were! It was as if someone had bewitched them (3:1).

Reader, are you doing what the Galatians were doing? Has the ground of your hope been shifting? Are you no longer looking exclusively to the Lord Jesus and his work on behalf of sinners? Is your reliance for acceptance with God now being shared between the Saviour and different kinds of works? Then, shocking as it may sound, you are doing what the Galatians were doing! You are deserting the God who so graciously called you. You need to pay urgent heed to the message of this letter!

The seriousness of preaching this 'different' gospel

In verse 8, in thunderous language, Paul leaves us in no doubt as to what an immensely serious matter it is to *preach* this 'different' gospel: 'But even if we or an angel from heaven should preach a gospel other than the one we preached to you, let him be eternally condemned!' And then he repeats it in verse 9: 'As we have already said, so now I say again: If anybody is preaching to you a gospel other than what you accepted, let him be eternally condemned!'

The word translated by the NIV as 'eternally condemned' is the Greek word *anathema*. In the Greek translation of the book of Joshua, it was used of the things and people of Canaan that were under the divine curse and devoted to destruction. Paul's desire was that this divine destruction would come upon the perverters of the gospel—so serious was their error. And he would admit no exceptions: whether the preacher should be an angel from heaven or the apostle Paul himself, the same judgement was invoked.

James Denney has some helpful comments on Paul's language here:

> The man who perverts [the gospel] is the worst enemy of God and man; and it is not bad temper or narrow-mindedness in St Paul which explains this vehement language, it is the jealousy of God which has kindled in a soul redeemed by the death of Christ a corresponding jealousy for the Saviour ... To touch [Paul's] teaching here is not to do something which leaves his gospel unaffected; ... it is to wound his gospel mortally.[4]

We are not warranted in concluding from this that those who preach a version of this 'different' gospel will certainly *be* condemned. God has been merciful to many a preacher who in the first days of his ministry has ignorantly preached salvation by works. God has opened his eyes to his error, and ever afterwards the man has preached the true gospel.

Where there is no repentance, however, and the preacher continues to insist that a religion of good works is the way to heaven, the curse of God will ultimately fall. Such a man has led his hearers far astray. He has fatally distorted the one message that tells them how to get right with God. He has helped to shut people out of heaven. And God, in righteous judgement, will respond by shutting such a man out of heaven.

So don't listen to them!

Paul's anxiety here is to break the hold these false teachers have over the minds of the Galatians. These are not the kinds of men they should be taking as their spiritual guides! And neither should we. Such men may be popular, gifted, eloquent, influential, and learned, and they may occupy high ecclesiastical office, but we are not to be dazzled. The critical question is: What is their message, their *gospel*? If it is not the gospel of God's grace that we find in the pages of the New Testament but a different gospel, we need to reject these teachers—and their message with them.

FOR FURTHER STUDY

1. In addition to the texts cited in this chapter, what evidence can you find in the New Testament for the divine authority with which Paul and his fellow apostles spoke and wrote?

2. Christ's deity lies at the foundation of the togetherness with God the Father illustrated in Paul's introduction. In what other ways does the New Testament teach this fundamental truth about the person of Christ?

TO THINK ABOUT AND DISCUSS

1. In what kinds of ways will our deliverance from this present evil age (1:4) show itself if it has really taken place?

2. Paul was astonished that the Galatians had so quickly begun to turn away from the truth. What can make a false gospel like the one the Galatians heard so attractive? What can make the men who preach it so believable? How are we to protect ourselves and others from doing what the Galatians had begun to do?

2 A message from heaven

(1:11–2:10)

Paul's gospel was certainly very different from that of his opponents in Galatia, but it was *not* different from that of his fellow apostles. These men stood shoulder to shoulder in proclaiming to Jews and Gentiles alike the same heaven-sent message.

'Interesting, useful, but now largely forgotten'—many a preacher's autobiography could be described in just such words. But not this man's! The apostle Paul was a preacher, and in the section of his letter extending from 1:11 to 2:10 he tells the Galatians a little of his story. And it is still going around the world! This fragment of a preacher's autobiography continues to be read everywhere, and not just by fellow preachers.

But why did Paul write these things? And why, if we are not preachers ourselves, is it worth listening to his story and endeavouring to learn it? Read on!

Before he was a preacher (1:13–14)

The apostle begins his story in verses 11 and 12 with a word or two about his *message* as a preacher. It is the single most important thing that he has to say, and he puts it first for emphasis. For our purposes, however, we are going to take it up in the middle of this section and begin instead with what Paul tells us about his life *before* he became a preacher: 'For you have heard of my previous way of life in Judaism, how intensely I persecuted the church of God and tried to destroy it. I was advancing in Judaism beyond many Jews of my own age and was extremely zealous for the traditions of my fathers' (vv. 13–14).

Paul's attitude towards the church was the very opposite of 'live and let live'. In his zeal for the Judaism to which he was so devotedly attached, he endeavoured to crush the church out of existence. It was, he says, his 'way of life' (v. 13). 'Hunting Christians', writes Leon Morris, 'was not a sideline when he had nothing else to occupy him. For Paul in these days to be alive was to be hunting Christians.'[1]

Becoming a preacher (1:15–16)

This being so, how likely was it that Paul should become both a Christian himself and a preacher of the gospel? From a human point of view, there was nothing *less* likely! And yet, in astonishing grace, that is exactly what happened! 'God, who set me apart from birth and called me by his grace, was pleased to reveal his Son in me that I might preach him among the Gentiles' (vv. 15–16).

We notice how pronouncedly the emphasis falls upon

what *God* did. It was God who *set him apart from birth*, literally, from his mother's womb. Something similar is said of Jeremiah the prophet (Jer. 1:4–5). We begin to look for a suitable person when a particular post needs to be filled, but that is not God's method. He chooses the workers and appoints them to their tasks before they are even born. All our God-given work is work that we were destined to do from the beginning of life.

Further, *God called him by his grace*. Usually in the New Testament, to be called is to be more than just invited. It is to be so acted upon by the grace of God that we are enabled to believe the gospel. Paul's conversion was to be traced to just such a calling. Wedded as he was to another religion, deeply antagonistic as he was to Christianity, he was not, however, beyond the reach of a gracious, life-transforming divine call. And neither is that unbeliever who is so much upon your heart.

> Usually in the New Testament, to be called is to be more than just invited. It is to be so acted upon by the grace of God that we are enabled to believe the gospel.

Finally, *God was pleased to reveal his Son in him*. This is a reference to inward illumination. To adapt the apostle's language in 2 Corinthians 4, the God who said, 'Let light shine out of darkness' made his light shine in Paul's heart to give him the light of the knowledge of the glory of God in the face of Jesus Christ (2 Cor. 4:6). As a result, Paul came to know not only *the truth* about God's Son, but actually to know *him*. It was this that fitted him to preach Christ. Nothing less than this is needed for preaching him today.

His movements as a preacher (1:17–24)

The remainder of Galatians 1 is taken up with some of Paul's initial movements as a preacher. It might have been expected that he would return to Jerusalem after his conversion and spend some time in the company of the apostles, learning from them about his new-found faith. Instead, he 'went immediately into Arabia' (v. 17). Though the reason for this has not been disclosed, it was in all likelihood for prolonged study, meditation, and communion with the Saviour.

When, after three years, he did go up to Jerusalem, it was for the purpose of making Peter's acquaintance. In the course of the visit he saw no other apostle except James, the Lord's brother. His stay was short—just fifteen days—and then, as we learn from Acts 9, it was necessary for him to be sent away for his safety. Later, as he tells us in verses 21–22, he went to Syria and Cilicia.

Why does Paul relate these things, solemnly swearing, in verse 20, that he is not lying? The answer is probably along the following lines: the false teachers who had come to Galatia and who had brought a different gospel with them had necessarily to explain how Paul had got *his* gospel wrong. And here is how they likely did it: by alleging that he had misunderstood it! He had failed to fully grasp the message committed to him by the other apostles. Hence the necessity of his mistakes being corrected.

If this *was* what they were saying, it explains why Paul recounted his early movements as a preacher. Whatever his message was, it was not some mangled version of what he had learned from the other apostles—he hadn't been around the other apostles to ever be instructed by them! Their paths and his, in God's providence, had been quite separate. As we learn from Galatians 2, it wasn't in fact until fourteen years after his conversion that he had any prolonged consultation with the other apostles, and by that time his gospel was 'fully developed'.[2]

His message as a preacher (1:11–12)

How, then, *did* Paul get his message? It is the very first thing that he tells us in this section: 'I want you to know, brothers, that the gospel I preached is not something that man made up. I did not receive it from any man, nor was I taught it; rather, I received it by revelation from Jesus Christ' (vv. 11–12). Just as man had nothing to do with Paul's apostolic *appointment* (v. 1), neither did he have anything to do with his apostolic *message*. It came to him directly from heaven. In Damascus and Arabia, the same Christ who had taught the Twelve, who after the resurrection had opened their minds to understand the Scriptures and who had poured out the Holy Spirit in order to lead them into all truth, now took Paul 'under his own immediate tuition'.[3] It was the substance of *this* instruction that Paul had preached in Galatia.

The divine origin of Paul's message means, for one thing, that the all-too-common charge against him of misrepresenting Christ and giving birth to a Christianity very different from what Christ intended is utterly without foundation. We cannot drive a wedge between Paul and

Christ—not when the apostle's message was given to him by Christ in the first place.

Beyond that, the divine origin of Paul's gospel makes it the yardstick by which we measure every claimant to be a message from heaven. Is it the message that *Paul* preached? If not, then it is not the gospel of Christ and therefore not the *true* gospel. It is a counterfeit, and because of that is neither to be preached by us nor believed. It is to be rejected.

Contending with men who disagreed with his message (2:4–5)

This divinely given message is at the heart of the events that Paul goes on to record for us in the opening ten verses of Galatians 2. We begin with verses 4–5, where we find the apostle contending with certain men who *disagreed* with him about his gospel: 'some false brothers had infiltrated our ranks to spy on the freedom we have in Christ Jesus and to make us slaves. We did not give in to them for a moment, so that the truth of the gospel might remain with you.'

There is some uncertainty as to exactly where and when these events took place. It is possible that the scene was Jerusalem during the visit described in the previous and succeeding verses. The grammar is so peculiar, however, that the reference is possibly to something that took place elsewhere and which occasioned the apostolic conference in the first place. Either way, Paul found himself in contention with these men.

He describes them as 'false brothers' (v. 4), men who were evidently Christian by profession but certainly not in truth. The underlying Greek word signifies 'one who pretends to be a Christian brother but whose claim is belied by his unbrotherly conduct'.[4] They were sham Christians, Christians in name only.

These false brothers are charged with infiltrating the ranks of the Christian brotherhood in order to spy on their freedom in Christ and make them slaves. We need to note carefully the word 'freedom' (v. 4). It is one of the key words in Galatians.

> Faith alone in Christ alone is all that is necessary, and to say otherwise is to attempt to make slaves of those whom God has set free.

One aspect of it is that Christ has released his people from all obligation to obey the Law of Moses. Apart from those elements of the law that have the character of the timeless and the universal, such as the Ten Commandments, Mosaic legislation is no longer binding. Contrary to what these false brothers appear to have been teaching, there is no need to be circumcised and to obey the law in order to be part of the new-covenant community and enjoy the riches of new-covenant blessing. Faith alone in Christ alone is all that is necessary, and to say otherwise is to attempt to make slaves of those whom God has set free. Paul would rightly have none of it: 'We did not give in to them for a moment, so that the truth of the gospel might remain with you' (v. 5).

These false brothers have their modern counterparts, and they are no less dangerous and no less in need of being opposed. If we are believers, a full pardon for sin and a righteousness that secures us eternal life are already ours—granted to us as a gift the moment we trusted the Saviour. And we enslave ourselves—we allow ourselves to be enslaved—when we begin to take on board the notion that faith in Christ is not sufficient and that it must be supplemented by certain works and religious ceremonies in order for us to be sure of being right with God. The warning of Galatians is that Christians can be lured by such teaching. Its message is that we must resist it.

Conversing with men who agreed with his message (2:1–10)

Galatians 2:1–10 is largely taken up with a visit Paul made to Jerusalem 'Fourteen years later' (v. 1)—these years being counted either from his previous visit or from his conversion. Some scholars have argued that this is the visit recorded in Acts 15, but it is more likely to be the one of which Luke writes in Acts 11. In the course of this visit, Paul had a meeting with 'those who seemed to be leaders' (v. 2), identified later in the passage (v. 9) as the apostles James, Peter, and John. At this meeting Paul privately set before them the gospel he had been preaching among the Gentiles, 'for fear', he says, 'that I was running or had run my race in vain' (v. 2).

What on earth does he mean? Surely after all these years Paul did not think that somehow he had got it wrong! John Stott helpfully explains,

> It was not, we may be sure, that he had any personal doubts or misgivings about his gospel and needed the reassurance of the other Jerusalem apostles, for he had been preaching it for fourteen years; but rather lest his ministry past and present should be rendered fruitless by the Judaizers [the name traditionally given to the Galatian errorists]... It was to overthrow their influence, not to strengthen his own

convictions that he laid his gospel before the Jerusalem apostles.[5]

This was a crisis time! With whom would these leaders side? Would they make common cause with Paul and unite against the opponents? In two very practical ways the Jerusalem apostles showed that they stood shoulder to shoulder with Paul.

The first was by *the acceptance of Titus*. When Paul went up to Jerusalem, he 'took Titus along also' (v. 1). Because Titus was a Greek (v. 3) and had therefore never been circumcised, he constituted a test case. What would be the attitude of the Jerusalem leaders? Would they seek to compel him to be circumcised (thereby siding with Paul's opponents)? Or would they accept him as a brother in Christ (as Paul had done) simply on account of his faith in Christ?

The apostles' decision, which to Paul's joy was to accept Titus as he was, helped set the direction for the church's entire future. It was not to be a *Jewish* body, to belong to which you needed to effectively become Jewish by submitting to the Jewish law. It was instead to be a *mixed* body, membership of which was open to people of all races simply on the basis of faith in Jesus Christ.

The second way in which the Jerusalem apostles showed their solidarity with Paul was by *the acceptance of Paul himself*. We learn from verses 6–10 that the Jerusalem apostles found nothing defective about the gospel Paul preached. They had no modifications to make to it. It was the same gospel which they themselves preached. The only difference that they recognized between themselves and Paul had to do with their respective spheres of operation. *Their* primary task (especially Peter's) was the preaching of the gospel to the Jews; Paul's, by contrast, was the preaching of the gospel to the Gentiles. So the Lord had ordered it. And we see in verse 9 that James, Peter, and John gave practical expression to their conviction on this point by giving to Paul and Barnabas the right hand of fellowship.

Harmony

We return now to the basic issue. Were the false teachers in Galatia saying that Paul's gospel was defective because he had distorted what he learned from the original apostles? How completely that accusation is refuted by this long section of the letter! Not only had Paul's gospel not come from his fellow apostles (but instead directly from Jesus), but also, when after many years they eventually compared notes on the matter, Paul and the other apostles were completely in agreement! There was no question as to who was siding with whom in this controversy. By their acceptance of Titus and of Paul himself the Jerusalem leaders sided with *Paul*! Justification by faith apart from the works of the law was their message too. On the fundamental question of what the gospel is, these men were of one heart and one mind.

A great lesson

It is unity of this kind that alone enables us to be partners in the gospel today. Like Paul and his brother apostles, we must be one in the fundamentals of the gospel—salvation by grace alone, through faith alone, in Christ alone. Where such unity is absent we cannot cooperate. We cannot stand shoulder to shoulder with men, organizations, or churches that are in error in regard to what the gospel basically is. We cannot support them financially, join with them in their efforts at outreach, pray for their success, or, in the interests of presenting a united front to the world, cover over our differences with a form of words that gives the erroneous impression that we are really one.

But where there *is* unity in the gospel, partnership is not only possible, it is altogether desirable. It enables Christians of different denominations to cooperate in home and foreign missions, in Bible translation and distribution, in the publication of Christian literature, in the training of men for the ministry, in the establishment of Christian schools, and in the preaching of the gospel. There are secondary issues on which we differ, but in regard to the heart of the gospel we are one.

FOR FURTHER STUDY

1. What other indications are there in Scripture that, as in the cases of Paul and Jeremiah, God has planned out the work that he has for us to do for him before our lives begin? What evidence is there that this pre-planning is not confined to the good works of God's own people but extends to the activities of the wicked?

2. How would you show from the New Testament that to be *called* usually means to be more than simply invited? What are some of the exceptions?

TO THINK ABOUT AND DISCUSS

1. Can you think of some contemporary examples of the kind of enslaving teaching that Paul is opposing in Galatians 2:4–5? Why is it that Christians can be lured by this kind of teaching?

2. At the end of the chapter, some suggestions were given of ways in which those who share a basic oneness in the gospel can fruitfully give expression to that oneness. In what other ways can ministers, local congregations, associations, or denominations do this?

3 A clash of apostles

(2:11–21)

To be discerning enough to see when an influential believer is in error and to be courageous enough to confront him or her about it are important qualities in a Christian leader. In this passage, Paul displays them both.

The resurrection of Christ and the outpouring of the Spirit on the Day of Pentecost impacted the apostle Peter profoundly. Without those events he would not have been the powerful evangelist and outstanding church leader that we see in Acts and in his own inspired letters. They did not, however, make him perfect. Weakness and sinfulness remained. The incident recorded in the latter part of Galatians 2 furnishes melancholy proof of that.

His behaviour at the beginning (v. 12)

The scene is Antioch, the chief city of Syria, the place where the first Gentile church had been planted and where the disciples were first called 'Christians'. These disciples have a distinguished guest! The apostle Peter has come on a visit, and at the outset (v. 12) he is happy to eat with them—presumably both at their common meals and at the Lord's Supper.

We must not overlook what a revolution in Peter's thinking this represented. In days gone by he, as a conscientious Jew, would have considered it wrong to eat with Gentiles on account of the ceremonial defilement that he risked contracting. But everything changed through a remarkable vision that he had, the details of which are recorded in Acts 10. By means of that vision, God taught him that the old distinction between clean and unclean foods was now abolished and that he must not consider *people* unclean on account of the things they ate. The result was first Peter's visit to the house of the Gentile Cornelius (Acts 10) and later his willingness to eat with the Gentile believers in Antioch.

His behaviour later on (vv. 11–14)

Sadly, things changed. When 'certain men came from James … he began to draw back and separate himself from the Gentiles because he was afraid of those who belonged to the circumcision group' (v. 12). If these visitors are the same ones of whom we read in Acts 15 (which is very likely), they were Jews who professed to be Christians, who came to Antioch without apostolic authorization (Acts 15:24), and who were insisting that if Gentiles were to be saved they needed to be circumcised and obey the Law of Moses. In effect, Gentiles needed to become Jews and to live like Jews—part of which meant that they could only eat food that according to Jewish law was ceremonially clean. Until they did so, it was improper and defiling for a Christian Jew to eat with them.

Amazingly, Peter gave in to these men and began to 'draw back and separate himself' from his Gentile brethren. And it was not because his convictions had changed; it was out of *fear* of these visitors, a fear that is not explained. The situation worsened when the other Jewish Christians in Antioch, including Barnabas, joined him (v. 13). Seeing what was happening, Paul could not remain silent: 'in front of them all' (v. 14), 'I opposed [Peter] to his face, because he was clearly in the wrong' (v. 11).

Justification (vv. 14–21)

It is evident from what Paul said to Peter in verses 14–16 that this withdrawing from Gentile believers was no small issue. His conduct was out of line with the truth of the gospel (v. 14), the gospel that declares 'that a man is not justified by observing the law, but by faith in Jesus Christ' (v. 16).

The word *justified*, which Paul uses three times in verse 16, is without question one of the most important words in the Bible. The sixteenth-century German Reformer Martin Luther, for example, said of it: 'This is the truth of the gospel. It is also the principal article of all Christian doctrine, wherein the knowledge of all godliness consisteth. Most necessary is it, therefore, that we should know this article well, teach it unto others, and beat it into their heads continually.' Again, he said, '… if the article of justification be lost, then is all true Christian doctrine lost.' Most memorably of all, he described it as '*articulus stantis vel cadentis ecclesiae*'—'the article of faith that decides whether the church is standing or falling'.[1]

There is nothing said in verses 14–16 about the *meaning* of the word. As we listen to the one apostle addressing the other, it is obvious that they both understood what justification is, for Paul didn't think it necessary to pause and explain it to Peter. It is likely, however, that not every reader of these words is in the same position. Also, since in the theological world of our day the meaning of justification is hotly disputed, some words of explanation will be good for us all.

The matter being addressed in justification is that of our standing before God in relation to his holy law—specifically the radical *alteration* in standing that believers in Christ come to enjoy. We begin with how it ought to be in *human* law courts. Moses says in Deuteronomy 25:1, 'When men have a dispute, they are to take it to court and the judges will decide the case, acquitting [literally, "justifying"] the innocent and condemning the guilty.' Judges—if they are doing their job properly—justify the innocent. They find them not guilty of the charges brought against them, judicially declare it to be so, and treat them accordingly by granting them their freedom. And if they don't—if instead they condemn the innocent and justify those who are guilty—they are declared by Scripture to be 'an abomination to the LORD' (Prov. 17:15, ESV).

It is this that makes God's justification of sinners so astonishing, for the very thing that he condemns in others he himself does, righteous God though he is. He justifies the ungodly. He finds in their favour, granting them the standing before his holy law of *righteous* men and women, and treats them accordingly. He makes them wholly free from condemnation and heirs instead of eternal life.

Justification and works of the law

Were God to do this by simply ignoring our great guilt he would be acting no less unrighteously than a judge who justifies guilty men or women in a human law court. But our guilt is not ignored. Behind God's justifying of sinners lies the perfect life and atoning death of Jesus, a life and death which have secured *righteousness* for us. And when that righteousness becomes ours, God is able, in perfect justice, both to pardon all our sins and to constitute and treat us as innocent before his law.

> Behind God's justifying of sinners lies the perfect life and atoning death of Jesus, a life and death which have secured *righteousness* for us.

One of the great concerns of Galatians is with *how* this righteousness becomes ours. How does God justify us? In Paul's reproof of Peter that question is answered both positively and negatively. Negatively, 'a man is not justified by observing the law' (Gal. 2:16). Later in the same verse the point is made twice more: '... not by observing the law, because by observing the law no one will be justified'. Literally, justification is not by 'works of law', an expression that has both a narrow and a broad reference. From different parts of Galatians we gather that there were three specific areas of law-keeping that the Galatian Christians had come to believe were binding on them for justification—circumcision, Old

Testament food laws, and Old Testament holy days. Paul is emphatic that it is not by submitting to such laws that the blessing of justification becomes ours.

Works of law, however, go way beyond the three named specifics. They cover all that God has ever laid down as law for mankind. They embrace all that is distinctively Mosaic; they embrace, too, those timeless and universal laws that are binding on us simply as human beings. This is particularly clear in Romans 1–3. It is not by obedience to *any* part of God's law that the blessing of justification becomes ours.

The negative needs to be understood no less today than in Paul's day. So many imagine that their endeavours to please God by keeping his law are what will gain them a favourable verdict on the Day of Judgement. It is not so. The eternally unchanging fact that we have sinned closes that door in our face. The language could not be less ambiguous: by observing the law *no one* will be justified. Rather, 'through the law we become conscious of *sin*' (Rom. 3:20, emphasis added).

Justification by faith

How, then, are we to be justified? Paul says, 'by faith in Jesus Christ' (Gal. 2:16); '… we, too,' he continues, 'have put our faith in Christ Jesus that we may be justified by faith in Christ.' The right way is as clearly indicated as the wrong. The blessing of justification becomes ours as we abandon all hope of ever being justified by our works and rely wholly upon Christ. We are to look to *him* and to him *alone*. As we do so, we are justified. Christ's perfect righteousness, wrought for us by his sinless life and sacrificial death, is imputed to us: it is put down to our account. And on that basis, God marvellously alters our status as sinners. He pardons all our sins and for ever reckons us, for Christ's sake, to be as innocent before his law as Christ himself.

Justification and Christian fellowship

It is against the background of this doctrine of justification—a doctrine on which both Peter and Paul were agreed—that we can appreciate why Paul reacted so strongly to Peter's behaviour. By withdrawing from his Gentile brothers, Peter had aligned himself with men who, by insisting that works of law were necessary for justification, were denying the Christian standing of these Gentiles. How could he do that? These men, as believers in Christ, were as fully Christian as Peter was. Peter knew that. How, then, could he withdraw from them and insist that they live as Jews before he would acknowledge them as his brothers? His conduct was clearly out of line with the gospel!

This incident is not as remote from us as it may seem. There are many differences among the justified. Their race can be different. So, too, the colour of their skin. There are often cultural differences, social differences, and differences on points of doctrine. They may belong to very different churches. Nevertheless, if they are believers in Jesus they are *justified*. And, according to Galatians 2, the relations of all other Christians towards them are to be shaped by that reality.

John Stott puts it like this: 'If *God* has accepted them, how can we *reject* them? If he receives them to *his* fellowship, shall we deny them *ours*? He has reconciled them to *himself*; how can we withdraw from those whom God has reconciled?'[2]

However many differences there may be between ourselves and other Christians (and there may be very many), the shared blessing of justification makes us *one*. In our relations with them we ought to give practical expression to that unity; welcoming them to the Lord's Table is a case in point. God has accepted every believer in Jesus, simply because he or she is a believer. Our doctrine of justification challenges us to make that visible by doing the same.

> However many differences there may be between ourselves and other Christians (and there may be very many), the shared blessing of justification makes us *one*.

Justification and Christian lifestyle

The closing verses of Galatians 2 have their difficulties. Their basic thrust, however, seems clear. A justified sinner may be free from the Mosaic law, but he or she may not and does not take that as a licence to sin. Was this one of the objections to Paul's teaching that the visitors to Antioch and the false teachers in Galatia were raising? It was certainly raised by others. If all at once, at the moment of faith, our sins are pardoned and we are unalterably put right with God, is that not an encouragement to sin? In an exquisitely beautiful piece of spiritual autobiography Paul answers both for himself and for every other true believer: 'I have been crucified with Christ and I no longer live, but Christ lives in me. The life I live in the body, I live by faith in the Son of God, who loved me and gave himself for me' (v. 20).

Before we became Christians, sin had us in its grip, shaping and determining the way that we thought and lived. It was in order to change this that the Son of God lovingly gave himself. He died for us so that we too might die—die, that is, to the sin that had controlling influence over us. And when we came to be united with him at the outset of our Christian lives, that was the very thing that happened. Paul uses astonishing language to describe it; he says, 'I have been crucified with Christ.' By virtue of his union with the Christ who had been crucified, he, too, had been crucified. Union with Christ meant *death* for him! It is the same for every believer. There is a death-dealing power that flows into us when we come to be united to Christ and its target is the old sin-dominated, God-excluding life that up until then we have been living. The target is not missed!

> Christ is the secret of those desires after God—that delight in his Word, that hatred of sin, that obedience to God's will—that were all so tragically absent from the old life.

Union with Christ, however, brings not only death to the believer but also new life, a life that is marked by the presence of Christ and by faith. For one thing, the believer can say with Paul, 'Christ lives in me'. What a difference he makes! Just as the presence of a particular individual in a school, company, or political party can radically alter things for the better, so also does the presence of Christ in a believer's heart. He is the secret of those desires after God—that delight in his

Word, that hatred of sin, that obedience to God's will—that were all so tragically absent from the old life.

The believer can also say with Paul that 'The life I live in the body, I live by faith in the Son of God'. By his presence in us, Christ is, as it were, holding onto us. And by faith we, for our part, are holding onto him. We abide in him, looking to him constantly to supply us with what we need for the living of our Christian lives, to be to us all that we need for righteousness and eternal life.

The truly justified, then, do not—indeed cannot—turn their wonderful new status into a licence to sin. For the truly justified are in union with Christ; we are 'justified *in Christ*' (v. 17, emphasis added). This union has brought such a radical death and new life to us that the inevitable upshot is a lifestyle characterized by holiness.

Justification and the cross

The chapter ends with Paul returning to the offensive: 'if righteousness could be gained through the law, Christ died for nothing!' (v. 21). His Galatian readers were being hoodwinked into thinking that the blessing of justification could only be theirs through observing the law. 'If that is indeed the way of justification,' Paul is saying, 'then Christ need not have bothered dying.' Why did he need to come from heaven and suffer and die if we could make it to heaven by our own good works? It is precisely because justification by works of law is an *impossibility* that the Son of God gave himself for us. His cross is the measure of our helplessness and our one effectual cure.

For further study ▶

1. If the resurrection of Christ and the outpouring of the Spirit on the Day of Pentecost did not make Peter perfect, what differences *did* they make to him?

2. Peter failed in the area of courage. What are some of the exhortations to be courageous that we find addressed to leaders of God's people in the Bible?

3. Galatians 2:20 points to the change that has taken place in us if we have been united to Christ. What other passages of Scripture point to the same change?

4. What evidence can you find in the New Testament that Peter did not hold a grudge against Paul for publicly opposing him?

TO THINK ABOUT AND DISCUSS

1. In what ways can a Christian leader fail, as Peter did, in the area of courage?

2. In addition to fellowship at the Lord's Table, what are some of the ways in which our common enjoyment of justification should show itself in our relations with other Christians? What are some of the barriers to be overcome, and how are they to be overcome?

3. How would you counsel someone who claimed to be justified but whose lifestyle gave no evidence of having been changed?

4 The importance of faith

(3:1–14)

There is a golden thread that binds the various parts of this passage together and gives them their unity: *faith*. Over against the false teaching that was persuading the Galatians to rely upon observing the law, Paul insists that, from start to finish, saving blessing comes to us through faith in Christ.

The apostle was aghast at the Galatians' folly (v. 1). Their conduct seemed incredible to him. It was as if they had been bewitched (v. 1), as if some evil power had cast a spell over them. They had taken teaching to heart which, on hearing, they should have instantly put away from them. The warmth and vigour of Paul's response to them is intended by God both to correct and prevent similar folly among professing Christians today.

What they had seen (vv. 1–2)

We learn from Paul's first letter to the Corinthians that the cross of Calvary was right at the heart of the message he preached in Corinth: 'I resolved to know nothing while I was with you except Jesus Christ and him crucified' (1 Cor. 2:2). It was the same in Galatia: 'Before your very eyes Jesus Christ was clearly portrayed as crucified' (Gal. 3:1). As one writer has paraphrased it, '… the message of Jesus as Messiah who died on the cross was plastered up on the bill-boards before your very eyes.'[1]

Interestingly, Paul did not elaborate but moved on immediately to a question about the Galatians' reception of the Holy Spirit (v. 2). He evidently considered the very reminder of what they had been shown of Christ crucified to be enough to bring home to them their foolishness. He had preached a Christ whose atonement was sufficient for their deliverance from sin. So perfect had been his Calvary work that nothing remained for anyone to do but to look to him in faith. And the Galatians had understood that and, by grace, had believed. Why, then, had their convictions and conduct changed? Why had they allowed themselves to be influenced by men whose doctrine of justification by works of law was so utterly subversive regarding the cross as to make it an unnecessary event (2:21)? It was folly!

Here Paul would teach us a lesson of *clarity*. Every preacher should be at pains, as Paul was, not only to set the cross before his hearers as the only and all-sufficient remedy for sin, but to do so *clearly*. More importantly, he would teach us a lesson of *fidelity*. Having seen the crucified Saviour as our one hope of salvation and looked to him in faith for forgiveness and righteousness, we must *go on* doing that. We must not repeat the folly of the Galatians by abandoning him and attempting to do the job ourselves.

What they had experienced (vv. 2–5)

In these verses Paul appeals to their experience, in particular, of the Holy Spirit. They had 'received' him (v. 2). He had come to them at the outset of their Christian lives, had brought them into the enjoyment of salvation in Christ, and now lived in their hearts for their sanctification, preservation, and empowerment for Christian service.

The critical question was: How had this happened? 'Did you receive the Spirit by observing the law, or by believing what you heard?' (v. 2). In verse 5, he repeats the question in slightly different words: 'Does God give you his Spirit and work miracles among you because you observe the law, or because you believe what you heard?' The Galatians knew the answer well! When they became Christians, they were strangers to the teaching which now so tragically attracted them. They had *Paul* as their preacher, and Paul had directed them to *Jesus*. And when they *believed* on Jesus, they received the Holy Spirit.

Why, then, the change? 'Are you so foolish? After beginning with the Spirit, are you now trying to attain your goal by human effort?' (v. 3). Evidently they were no longer feeling the helplessness they had felt at first and which had moved them to look to the *Lord* for salvation. They were looking instead to themselves and foolishly endeavouring to carry on and complete the work of salvation by their own efforts at obedience.

We are to learn from their folly. Our Christian lives must continue in exactly the same way that they began. How did *we* receive the Holy Spirit? Like the Galatians, not as a reward for our obedience but as a gift from God when we believed. It is on the same footing of grace and faith that we enjoy his *ongoing* ministry. That is never something earned. We do not perform acts of obedience to God's law and as a reward for that obedience secure the Spirit's powerful influences. Like Paul (2:20), we are to live by faith in the Son of God, looking to him dependently day by day for everything we need, whether it be forgiveness, justifying righteousness, or the work of the Spirit to make us holy.

A doctrine with a long history (vv. 6–9)

Paul will have more to say about the sanctifying ministry of the Spirit later in his letter. For now, it's back to justification and the critical role faith has in making that blessing ours. Specifically, in verses 6–9, he would have us understand that justification by faith is no new doctrine but one that has been around for a very long time indeed.

Justification lay, of course, at the heart of the Protestant Reformation of the sixteenth century. Its rediscovery transformed the life of Martin Luther and, in turn, through him and the other Reformers, the face of Europe. But justification by faith is no mere Reformation doctrine. The Reformers were at pains to show that what they were preaching was nothing more than what they had learned from the pages of the New Testament, especially from Paul's letters to the Romans and the Galatians.

The doctrine wasn't new, however, even in New Testament times. Certainly, greater light was shed on it through the death and resurrection of Jesus and by the outpouring of the Spirit. But the doctrine itself was already old in Paul's day—a point clearly established by the quotation in Galatians 3:6 from Genesis 15:6 that refers to Abraham: 'He believed God, and it was credited to him as righteousness.' The event in question had taken place some 2,000 years before. Way back then, Abraham, the father of the Jewish race, had been justified by faith.

The meaning of faith being credited for righteousness has been the subject of debate. And it is no mere academic debate, for, according to Romans 4, faith continues to be credited to believers for righteousness. Is Scripture saying (as some maintain) that faith is *itself* our righteousness? That, since it is not possible for us to attain righteousness by obedience to the law, God accepts faith as a kind of substitute or equivalent? Paul's teaching elsewhere about 'righteousness from God' that 'comes through faith ... to all who believe' (Rom. 3:22) and 'righteousness that comes from God and is by faith' (Phil. 3:9) points to a different solution. Faith and righteousness are not one and the same thing, but

> Faith and righteousness are not one and the same thing, but two distinct things, the one being the instrument by which the other is obtained.

two distinct things, the one being the instrument by which the other is obtained. The righteousness that is credited to the believer is a 'faith-righteousness', that is, a righteousness that comes into our possession by *means* of faith.

Well, this had been Abraham's experience, and the Galatians needed to lay the lesson of it to heart. It seems that the false teachers had seriously misled them by saying something like this: 'If you Gentiles want to belong to God, you need to become children of Abraham. You need to get into Abraham's family line so that the blessings of salvation promised to Abraham's offspring can be yours. The only way to do that is to be circumcised as Abraham was.'

Paul would have none of it: it is 'those who *believe*' who 'are children of Abraham' (v. 7, emphasis added). It was true that Abraham had been circumcised—but not until long after the events of Genesis 15. Abraham's circumcision had nothing to do with his justification. It was wholly a matter of faith laying hold upon God and his Word. That meant that, if the Galatians shared Abraham's faith, they were *already* his children and therefore heirs of all the saving blessing promised to his offspring. It is no different today. Those who enjoy salvation are Abraham's spiritual children (see Gal. 3:29), and have become such in exactly the same manner by which they have become the children of God: by *faith*.

A doctrine with a wide geography (v. 8)

Paul reminds us of something foreseen long ago by Holy Scripture: 'The Scripture foresaw that God would justify the Gentiles by faith, and announced the gospel in advance to Abraham: "All nations will be blessed through you" [a quotation from Genesis 12:3]' (v. 8).

The New Testament interprets this for us. A Saviour would come in Abraham's line. In and by the gospel he would be presented to all the nations as an object of saving faith, and people would believe in him and be justified. That is what was foreseen and announced. And it has happened! Justification by faith, the doctrine with a long history, has come to have, as it were, *a wide geography*. It is being preached in every corner of the globe, and wherever it goes it both announces rich blessing for sinners and communicates it to everyone who believes. It did so in Gentile Galatia. By faith in the Jesus whom Paul preached to them, the Galatians fell heirs to the same blessing of justification that Abraham enjoyed. It is no different today. All over the world, helpless sinners are hearing of a Saviour to whom they can go in their desperate need, a Saviour who pardons them and clothes them with his perfect righteousness the moment they believe in him.

Under the curse (vv. 10–12)

In order to bring home to his readers how grave a matter it was to be now observing the law for their justification, and how vital it was that they return to their former trust in the Saviour, the apostle solemnly announces in verse 10 that 'All who rely on observing the law'—that is, for justification—'are under a curse'. The curse in question is the penalty imposed by God for breaking his law, and Scripture is emphatic that no law-breaker is exempt from that curse: '… it is written [Deut. 27:26], "Cursed is *everyone* who does not continue to do *everything* written in the Book of the Law'" (v. 10, emphasis added).

It is perfectly true that this curse would hold no terrors for us if our obedience to God's law was perfect. When verse 12 quotes from Leviticus 18:5, 'The man who does these things will live by them', it is being admitted as a general principle that obedience to the law of God will issue in eternal life. The righteous God will certainly justify righteous people and treat them accordingly!

There is a universal problem, however. In Romans 3, Paul declares that 'Jews and Gentiles alike are all under *sin*' (Rom. 3:9), and that 'all have *sinned* and fall short of the glory of God' (v. 23, emphasis added). We are all *law-breakers*! The Jew has failed to keep the whole of the duties imposed in the Book of the Law, the Gentile to keep the great moral principles of that law which are written on his or her heart (Rom. 2:12–15). We are *all* under the curse! And that is why the insistence that we observe the law for justification is so utterly preposterous. It is to try to attain righteousness by the very law that condemns us, by a law that has justly placed us under a curse for our transgressions.

> We are all *law-breakers*! The Jew has failed to keep the whole of the duties imposed in the Book of the Law, the Gentile to keep the great moral principles of that law which are written on his or her heart.

Christ a curse for us (v. 13)

In what is without question one of the most remarkable statements in the New Testament on the death of Christ, Paul says in verse 13, 'Christ redeemed us from the curse of the law by becoming a curse for us—for it is written, "Cursed is everyone who is hanged on a tree"' (ESV). The cross was a scene of *redemption*, an idea with which Paul's first-century readers were more familiar than we are today. To redeem someone (a slave, for example) was to secure his or her freedom by the payment of a price. And it was in order to redeem *us*, to secure our freedom from the curse of the law, that Jesus died on Calvary.

What a price he paid for it! He redeemed us from the curse of the law, says Paul, by 'becoming a curse for us' (v. 13). The penalty of our law-breaking was transferred to him. For a wrath-deserving people he became the wrath-bearer, an accursed one, bearing the curse that should have been borne by us.

In confirmation of that, Paul quotes yet another Old Testament Scripture (Deut. 21:23): 'Cursed is everyone who is hanged on a tree.' When a criminal under Old Testament law was put to death by being hanged on a tree it pointed to the fact that he or she was under the curse of God. The nailing of Jesus to the cross symbolized the very same thing. Frequently in the New Testament the cross of Calvary is thought of and spoken of as a *tree* (Acts 5:30; 13:29; 1 Peter 2:24). That is because the Christ who died there was under the curse of God—redeeming us from the curse of the law by becoming a curse for us.

Deliverance from the curse (vv. 11, 14)

The apostle uses the language of accomplished fact. Christ

actually redeemed us at Calvary—there and then, by his substitutionary death, paying the necessary price for our deliverance from the curse of the law. The fruit of that event is a series of magnificent blessings that flow to those who make him the object of their trust.

One such blessing is *justification*. When Paul writes in verse 14 that 'He redeemed us in order that the blessing given to Abraham might come to the Gentiles through Christ Jesus', the reference is to the blessing of justification. Transgression and curse may mean that the way to that blessing by observing the law is firmly closed to us, but another way has been opened wide, the way of faith in the crucified Redeemer. Through believing in him there is both deliverance from the curse and enjoyment of the divine favour.

Another blessing is *eternal life*. 'Clearly no one is justified before God by the law, because, "The righteous will live by faith"' (v. 11, quoting Hab. 2:4). An alternative translation reads, 'He who through faith is righteous will live'. A connection is being drawn between faith, righteousness, and life. To experience the 'curse of the law' is to be subjected to death in the fullest and most awful sense—to be eternally separated from God, soul and body, in hell. To be delivered from the curse means the opposite experience—the blessing of eternal life.

The final blessing is *the gift of the Spirit*. 'He redeemed us ... so that by faith we might receive the promise of the Spirit' (v. 14). Through the redeeming work of Christ the transforming presence and ministry of the Holy Spirit, graciously promised beforehand, is given to every believer.

The importance of faith

The opening words of this chapter identified *faith* as the golden thread that binds the various parts of this passage together and gives them their unity. I trust that we have seen that to be so. For justification, membership of the family of Abraham, eternal life, the gift of the Holy Spirit, and the enjoyment of his ongoing work, we are not to look to the law but in faith to Christ. It is with him that we are to begin and with him that we are to continue. We are fools if we do otherwise.

For further study ▶

FOR FURTHER STUDY

1. Other than this section in Galatians, what evidence is there in the New Testament that the gift of the Spirit is given to us when we believe in Christ?

2. What are the elements of God's law of which people without the special revelation of the Bible have knowledge?

TO THINK ABOUT AND DISCUSS

1. How would you explain the 'bewitching' of 3:1? Does it imply the activity of the evil one? What role does the evil one play in the errors into which God's people fall?

2. What is the evidence that the doctrine of justification was not new in Abraham's day but was even then an old doctrine?

3. Why is it entirely appropriate for Paul in verse 8 to personify Scripture by speaking about it *foreseeing*?

4. How would you respond to the charge that a God who regards and treats people as accursed on account of their transgressions is not very loving?

5 The dawning of a new age

(3:15–4:7)

Some things didn't change with the coming of Christ. The old way of salvation by faith, for example, remained the same. But other things did change. The Mosaic era came to a close, its preparatory mission complete, and a new age dawned, bringing greater light, privilege, and blessing than had ever been enjoyed before.

Unlike their Jewish contemporaries, the Gentile Galatians had not grown up with the Law of Moses. They would, of course, have known of its existence and perhaps been familiar with certain of its tenets. Indeed, some of them—proselytes to the Jewish faith—would have been faithful observers of the law. For the most part, however, the law was not something with which as Gentiles they had previously had anything to do.

By the time Paul wrote his letter to them the situation had dramatically changed. If they had been strangers to the law in the past, they were certainly making up for it now. The

62

law had assumed massive importance for them. They now held themselves obligated to keep it and to do so in order to be saved.

As we have seen, this was an utterly *false* notion, and Paul's concern in the first section before us, 3:15–25, is (as it is in the letter as a whole) to dislodge it. These verses are all about the *law*, and Paul's purpose is to persuade his readers of a truth that each one of us needs to embrace and hold, namely, that the blessing of justification comes not through our efforts at obedience but through faith in Jesus.

Let's approach the section by picturing a house with several rooms. The house is called Law House and we will visit each room in turn, look around, and then move on to the next.

The law and the promise (3:15–19)

We discover in our first room that the Law of Moses made something of a late arrival on the scene. It was not until several centuries after God made a covenant with Abraham that the law was 'added' (v. 19), by which time Abraham's descendants had multiplied greatly. In verse 17 the time '430 years' is used, and a number of different suggestions have been made as to the precise period that they cover. For us it is enough to note that a very long time elapsed between the covenant with Abraham and the giving of the law.

This time period is very significant for Paul's argument. The dispute in Galatia (and it is still a dispute today) was over the basic matter of how sinners can come to be accepted by God as righteous. According to this passage, the question was settled long before the law was given when God made certain promises to Abraham.

These promises 'were spoken to Abraham and to his seed' (v. 16), 'his seed' being identified at the end of that verse as 'one person, who is Christ'. When God made his promises to Abraham he was, at the very same time, making them with the Christ who would afterwards come from Abraham. What those promises were has already been indicated in verses 8–14. They concern the blessings that would come to the world *through* Christ—the blessings of justification, life, and the Holy Spirit that would be conferred on all who believed.

The point to note here is that everything was settled centuries before the law came on the scene. A Saviour would come in Abraham's line. Through believing in him, people everywhere would be saved. And the law did nothing to alter that! It left the promises of God concerning salvation through faith wholly untouched.

The law and sin (3:19)

As we move into the second room we find the apostle asking and answering what, given the contents of the first room, is the obvious question: 'What, then, was the purpose of the law?' (v. 19). The remarkable answer is this: 'It was added because of transgressions.'

Paul's words in Romans 5:20 may very well explain his language here in Galatians 3. There he says that 'The law was added', not so that sin might be restrained (as we might expect), but 'so that the trespass might increase'. By multiplying the regulations that were to govern the people of God, the law, for one thing, vastly increased the *scope* for transgression. It also, on account of the perversity of the human heart, actually *stimulated* transgression. The very fact that the law forbade things prompted people to go ahead and do them.

Alternatively, in Galatians 3 Paul might be thinking about the *revelatory* power of the law. The law is like a mirror that shows us the extent of our sin. Either way, his explanation points up the Galatians' folly. We sometimes say of people that they couldn't have chosen a worse way to go about something. That is exactly what can be said of both the Galatians and their modern-day counterparts. What folly to seek justification by a law that, because of our depravity, occasions sin, stimulates sin, and brings sin to light!

The law and life (3:21–22)

What we see in the third room is no more pleasant than what we saw in the second. The principle stated earlier in verse 12, that 'The man who does these things [the things written in the law] will live by them', is great news for the perfect. If, without any deviation, we do the whole of what God requires of us, we will assuredly be blessed with eternal life.

When sin comes into the picture (as it has done in the case of us all), everything changes. There is no question as to the truth of Paul's assertion in verse 21: '... if a law had been given that could impart life, then righteousness would certainly have come by the law.' But no such law has been given. The only law there is stands before us as a mirror, showing us that we are sinners and condemning us. Hence the declaration of Scripture 'that the whole world is a prisoner of sin' (v. 22).

There is no way for any of us to righteousness and life by obedience to God's law when that very law condemns us for our sin.

The law and the Jews (3:23–25)

As we move into the fourth room, vivid glimpses are given to us of life under the law. What was it like for Jews to have to live in conformity to the whole Mosaic law?

Certainly it was not a wholly negative experience. From the Psalms, for example, it is clear that spiritual life could flourish under the law. Furthermore, the law's design was to protect the people by separating them in religion and practice from the corruptions of the surrounding nations. And finally, when there was obedience to the law, God poured out his blessing.

However, there was another side to it. In verse 23, for example, Paul speaks about the law locking people up and holding them prisoner. Then in verses 24–25 he speaks of the law being 'put in charge' and of the people being 'under the supervision of the law'. The underlying word in both of these phrases is *pedagogue*, the guardian appointed to serve as both a child's protector and disciplinarian until he or she came of age. It wasn't easy to be under the law, and it wasn't meant to be. With its multiplicity of regulations that served to multiply transgressions and increase the sense of sin, with its complex system of sacrifices that could never

> Life under the law was meant to be something from which God's people looked forward to being delivered.

effectively deal with sin, life under the law was meant to be something from which God's people looked forward to being delivered. It was temporary and preparatory, paving the way for the coming of something better.

The law and faith (3:23–25)

What that something better is we see in our fifth and final room. It contains the most splendid furniture, the centrepiece being the faith that 'has come' (v. 25). We must be careful not to misinterpret this. When Paul speaks in verse 23 about a time 'Before this faith came' and of being 'locked up until faith should be revealed', we are not to suppose that before the coming of Christ faith as the way of salvation was unknown. The reference in verse 6 to Abraham's faith, for example, disproves that at a stroke. Faith has always been the way by which sinners have come to be right with God.

> Faith has always been the way by which sinners have come to be right with God.

What is different in New Testament times is that faith has come to be explicitly fixed on the Jesus who came from heaven to live and die for us. It is he who is now faith's particular object. And with his coming, 'we are no longer under the supervision of the law' (v. 25). Certainly there is a carry-over of commandments into the new-covenant era—those elements of the Mosaic law that belong to the divine order of things for man as man (such as the Decalogue). But as a way of regulating the lives of God's chosen people, the Mosaic era is over. With Christ's coming, a *new* age has dawned.

How foolish the notion, then, that the Galatians needed to place themselves under the law! Not only had it *never* been the way to justification (that had always and only been by faith), it was not even any longer God's rule of life for his people. Everything had changed with Christ's appearing. The Galatians needed to look exclusively to *him* for their justification and regulate their Christian lives in accordance with his new-covenant instructions. We need to do the same.

New relationships (3:26–29)

In these verses the apostle touches on the remarkable new relationships into which our faith in Christ has introduced us.

The first to be mentioned is our new relationship with *God the Father*: 'You are all sons of God through faith in Christ Jesus' (v. 26). In his letter to the Ephesians Paul speaks about how God 'In love ... predestined us to be adopted as his sons through Jesus Christ, in accordance with his pleasure and will' (Eph. 1:5). God has purposed to make sinners his sons! When we come to faith in Christ that purpose is brought to fruition. We are not only justified, we are also adopted into God's family and have the privilege of being God's children.

Then there is our relationship with *Christ himself*. It is he who is the object of our faith (v. 26), and that faith brings us into the closest connection with him. It so unites us to him that in a mysterious but real way we actually come to be 'in' him (v. 28). In the language of verse 27, we 'clothe ourselves' with Christ (more literally, 'put on' Christ)—an act and reality symbolized in Christian baptism.

Faith also brings us into the closest of relationships with *every other believer*: 'There is neither Jew nor Greek, slave nor free, male nor female, for you are all one in Christ Jesus' (v. 28). So closely have we come to be joined to one another in Christ that we can be said to have become *one*. Since, quite apart from the Galatian controversy, this verse has been much discussed, I want to linger over it for a little while.

The answer to a deep dividedness

In a number of areas the world of Paul's day was deeply divided. At a racial level, for example, Jews despised Gentiles, speaking of them as 'dogs', while the typical Gentile had no less contempt for Jews. Socially, the great division was between slaves (of whom there were many millions) and freemen. And then there was the issue of gender: women were generally despised and treated as second-class citizens.

Against this background of deep dividedness—the reality of which in different ways remains with us still—we can appreciate the magnitude of what is being said here about the influence of the gospel. It straddles the divisions. People of every race, of every social class, men and women equally, are invited to come to the Saviour, and when they do, they are so fused into one that it is as if the differences dividing them no longer exist.

Abiding distinctions

We must not so read Paul as to make him the author of nonsense. For all the oneness that we enjoy in Christ, there are abiding distinctions. Jews remain Jews; men, men; women, women; and so on. Our in-Christness addresses the sin, the snobbery, the hostility, the exploitation, and the prejudice that cast such dark shadows over our human relations. But it does not make us the same.

Equality in saving blessing

In what sense, then, *are* we one? Or, to put it another way: How can we be *so* one in Christ that there is 'neither Jew nor Greek, slave nor free, male nor female'? The answer is that in Christ we are all raised to the same high level of saving privilege. We are *equally in Christ*, for instance. The poor believer is as fully united to his Saviour and as fully a participant in his life as the rich believer. We are also equally *the children of God*. No one in Christ is a mere cousin or distant relation; every believer is a son. God is as much the white believer's Father as he is the black believer's. Again, we are equally *the children of Abraham*: 'If you belong to Christ, then you are Abraham's seed' (v. 29), his spiritual offspring, independent of whether we are Jews or Gentiles. And finally, we are equally *heirs according to the promise* (v. 29). Abraham's spiritual seed were to have a spiritual inheritance, an inheritance that included justification, the gift of the Spirit, and the enjoyment of eternal life. Regardless of race, social rank, and gender, that inheritance is ours if we are believers in Jesus.

> No one in Christ is a mere cousin or distant relation; every believer is a son.

In the light of this, how terribly divisive was the teaching to which the Galatians had fallen prey! They were being told that as Gentile believers they had not yet been raised to the same level of privilege as Jewish believers. They were at best poor cousins, still outside the inner circle of blessing until they submitted to being circumcised. But no such division existed. Nor does it exist between believers of different race, social class, and gender today. We are, in the highest sense, *one*. And we must not permit that oneness to be threatened by racism, social snobbery, or demeaning attitudes towards those of the opposite sex, but instead be at pains to exhibit it in all our relations with one another.

The sending of God's Son (4:1–7)

The opening verses of Galatians 4 are admittedly difficult. It is unclear whether Paul is thinking about life under the law for the Jew (as he has been doing already), or life under the dark influences of pagan religion for the Gentile. Either way, his point is this: an event has taken place that has ushered in the greater liberty and richer privileges of the new-covenant era—the sending of God's Son. '[W]hen the time had fully come'—that is, the time set by the Father to introduce the gospel age—'God sent his Son, born of a woman, born under law' (v. 4).

His purpose in doing so was twofold. First, it was 'to redeem those under law'. By our law-breaking we were under the law's curse (3:10), the punishment due to us for our sins. God sent his Son (and later delivered him up to the death of the cross, 3:13) in order to *redeem* us from that curse. In his humanity, the Son subjected himself to both the law's demands and its penalties, that we might be freed from its condemnation.

Second, his purpose was 'that we might receive the full rights of sons' (v. 5). God's sending of his Son was so that the adoption to which we were lovingly predestined (Eph. 1:5) might become a reality for every believer (Gal. 3:26). Sonship could not become ours automatically—only through the incarnation and the cross. Now that it *has* become ours, we have, as a consequence, the Spirit of God's Son in our hearts and the privilege of being heirs (4:6–7).

It is the privilege of being heirs that forms the connecting link between this opening section of chapter 4 and the closing section of chapter 3. In Christ we are 'heirs according to the promise' (3:29), and in part that inheritance is already ours to enjoy. Already we are in a justified state, enjoy new life, and have Christ's Spirit in our hearts. But there is much more to come! God has only *begun* to show us what he has in store for us. The new age has merely *dawned*. The glory of high noon is yet before us.

For further study ▶

FOR FURTHER STUDY

1. What are some of the passages of Scripture that shed light on both the blessedness of the Mosaic era and its limitations?

2. In what ways do you as a new-covenant believer differ from a true believer of old-covenant days? In what ways are you the same?

TO THINK ABOUT AND DISCUSS

1. How would you show that the Ten Commandments are among those carried over from the Mosaic era into the new-covenant era? Is there other carry-over legislation you can identify?

2.How would you show from Scripture that notwithstanding our oneness in Christ men and women have distinct roles both in the church and in the home? What are those roles?

3. In what practical ways can oneness in Christ be exhibited in your congregation and the evils that divide be avoided?

4. The redemption of those under law (Gal. 4:5) cannot mean that we are now free from all obligation to obey God's law. Discuss why.

5. To what blessings will we fall heir when the dawn eventually gives way to the glory of high noon?

6 From slavery to freedom

(4:8–5:1)

Christians are not always free. Many in
apostolic times were enslaved to earthly
masters, and some are similarly enslaved today.
Christians can be citizens of enemy-occupied
nations or be locked up in prison for their faith.
Always, however, we are *spiritually* free in
Christ. Paul's concern is that we should guard
that freedom carefully and resist every attempt
to take it away.

D otted here and there in Paul's letters are
references to his journeys and labours as a
Christian missionary, and it is sometimes
possible to turn to the book of Acts for further
information. We cannot, however, do that with what he
tells us in Galatians 4:13: 'As you know, it was because of
an illness that I first preached the gospel to you.' Acts tells us
nothing about this illness and, with the possible exception of
2 Corinthians, nor do any of Paul's letters. In 2 Corinthians

Paul speaks about 'a thorn in my flesh' (2 Cor. 12:7) given to him to keep him from spiritual pride, and many have conjectured that this was the illness referred to in Galatians 4. It may be, but that's as certain as we can be. All we know is that, in the course of the missionary journey that took him to Galatia, Paul became ill, and it was *because* he became ill that he ended up preaching the gospel there.

How often this happens! The Lord brings sickness into a believer's life and it leads to opportunities to share the gospel that would not otherwise have arisen.

How he was received (4:8–15)

It would appear that the illness was unpleasant not only to Paul, but also potentially so to others. Verse 14 suggests, in fact, that the usual response in that culture was to treat the victim with contempt or scorn—perhaps because the illness caused disfigurement.

But it was not with contempt or scorn that the Galatians treated Paul. Anything but! '[Y]ou welcomed me as if I were an angel of God, as if I were Christ Jesus himself' (v. 14). 'I can testify', he continues, 'that, if you could have done so, you would have torn out your eyes and given them to me' (v. 15). These words perhaps imply that Paul was suffering from an eye complaint. Alternatively, they may simply be a colourful way of saying, 'You would have done anything to make me better!' Either way, the Galatians had taken him warmly to their hearts.

The reason why is not hard to discover. It lies in the message Paul preached to them and the impact of that message on their lives. It delivered them from slavery 'to those who by nature are not gods' (v. 8) and brought them instead to 'know God', or more especially, to be 'known by God' (v. 9). It introduced them into God's family (in v. 12 Paul addresses them as 'brothers') and evidently filled their hearts with joy (v. 15). The gospel did great things for them! Hence their affection for the man from whose lips the life-changing message had come.

Alienation (4:16–17)

Relationships between Christians can change, however, and not always for the better. It is apparent from Paul's question in verse 16 that the Galatians' affection for him had cooled considerably: 'Have I now become your enemy by telling you the truth?' What had happened? The answer is in verse 17. Referring to the false teachers who were causing such havoc, Paul writes, 'Those people are zealous to win you over, but for no good. What they want is to alienate you from us, so that you may be zealous for them.' In order to gain credence for their false gospel, it seems that the false teachers had said disparaging things about Paul (we noted this in the first chapter of the book). He was far less worthy of their respect as a spiritual teacher than they had supposed. Sadly, the Galatians had only too readily lent their ears to these false teachers, and the result was a rift.

Anxiety (4:8–10, 19–20)

Hurtful as this doubtless was to Paul, what was uppermost in his heart was a loving concern for the Galatians themselves. In verse 19 he calls them his 'dear children' and says that he is 'again in the pains of childbirth' for them. In the following verse he declares that he is 'perplexed' about them. Earlier, he has even gone so far as to express the fear that somehow he has wasted his efforts on them (v. 11). All personal considerations—and in this Paul is the model pastor—are swallowed up by his intense anxiety for them.

So what were they doing? 'You are observing special days and months and seasons and years!' (v. 10). The reference is to all the special events of the Jewish calendar, from the weekly seventh-day Sabbath to the Year of Jubilee. Gentiles as they were, they had taken them all on board and were observing them for their salvation. Faith in Jesus, they had been told, was not enough for justification. They had to effectively become Jews and begin to observe the Jewish calendar. They had started, too! And Paul is staggered: 'Do you not realize what you are doing?' he asks. 'You are enslaving yourselves all over again!'

When the apostle says in verse 8, 'Formerly, when you did not know God, you were slaves to those who by nature are not gods', the reference is to demons. Demons stood behind the old pagan rituals and by means of them enslaved the worshippers. And now, having been set free by Jesus, they were enslaving themselves all over again! Even though the Mosaic law had come from God, to adopt it as a means of getting right with God was to put themselves back under the same kind of slavery they had known in their unconverted days. 'As far as Paul was concerned—and this must have shocked the Judaizers—this kind of religion was no better than paganism.'[1]

So where, then, does true liberty lie? It lies in the privilege that is ours as believers to know God—indeed, to be known *by* God (v. 9). Through his Son, God has entered into a relationship of love and commitment to us, and we in turn have come to love and be committed to him. It was for just such mutual knowing that we were first created and then afterwards redeemed. We are not

> True liberty lies in the privilege that is ours as believers to know God—indeed, to be known *by* God.

required to labour for it by our efforts after obedience. It is already ours through our union with Christ. Our duty (and our wisdom) is simply to go on looking to him in faith to continue and to deepen it.

The allegory (4:21–5:1)

To further press home the warnings he has been giving them, Paul proceeds in the remaining part of the chapter to allegorize and apply a well-known story from the Old Testament. An allegory has been defined as 'a story in which specific people, places, and events stand for deep spiritual truth'.[2] The most famous example in Christian literature is Bunyan's *Pilgrim's Progress*. Now, between Bunyan's story and Paul's there is, of course, a big difference. Bunyan's tale is made up while Paul's is true. Nevertheless, there is a basic similarity. Both make the details of their stories pictures of spiritual truth.

Mothers and sons

'Father Abraham had many sons; many sons had Father Abraham.' So runs the children's chorus. At the beginning of *this* story, however, he had none. He had been married to Sarah for many years, but they had never been able to have children. Furthermore, it was now way past the time when such a thing was humanly possible, because Sarah was so old. Nevertheless, Abraham did eventually have two sons—Ishmael and Isaac—and through them, numerous descendants.

It is on these two sons and their respective mothers that the story centres. What happened was as follows: Sarah got to the point where she could stand being childless no longer and she decided to take matters into her own hands. She had a slave woman by the name of Hagar whom she took and gave to Abraham as a kind of secondary wife, so that through her Sarah might build a family. The upshot was that Abraham had a son by Hagar—*Ishmael*.

Years went by, and the unexpected and miraculous took place: Abraham had a son by Sarah. He was born, as Paul puts it at the end of Galatians 4:23, 'as the result of a promise'. God had said on a number of occasions that he would bless Abraham with numerous descendants, and it was this that he had in mind all along: to fulfil the promise through a son born to Sarah—*Isaac*.

The story, then, is of two sons and two mothers—Ishmael, the son of the slave woman, Hagar; and Isaac, the son of the free woman, Sarah. Basically, Paul sees two big pictures in the story.

A picture of spiritual slavery

Hagar the slave woman has a son who, by virtue of the fact that he is born of a slave, is a slave himself. It is a picture of *spiritual* slavery.

In tracing out the details of the picture we begin with verse 25: 'Hagar ... corresponds to the present city of Jerusalem, because she is in slavery with her children.' Here, as elsewhere, Jerusalem is a symbol of the nation of Israel as a whole. Paul is thinking about the Jews of his own day and is saying that they are in slavery. This had nothing to do with the Roman occupation. The slavery in question was a *spiritual* slavery and was to be traced to their gravely mistaken thinking about the Law of Moses given to them at Mount Sinai (vv. 24–25).

For one thing, they believed that the old covenant remained in force and that they were still bound to observe the law—even though, with the coming of Christ, God's way of relating to his covenant people had dramatically changed. More seriously, they were endeavouring by means of the law to attain to a justifying righteousness—a use to which God never intended it should be put. The result was a burdensome, lifelong, and yet ultimately futile pursuit of what the law could never give.

A picture of spiritual freedom

Sarah, the free woman, also had a son. By virtue of the fact that he was born of a free woman, Isaac was free himself. Paul wants us to see in this a picture of *spiritual* freedom.

In verse 26 mention is made of another Jerusalem, 'the Jerusalem that is above'. In contrast to the 'present Jerusalem' (the old-covenant community), this 'Jerusalem that is above' is the new-covenant community, that is, the New Testament church and her members. She is emphatically declared to be *free* (v. 26). By grace, believers in Jesus have entered into the new-covenant relationship God promised that his people would one day enjoy with him. God is now, in the highest sense of all, *our* God—the God who in entering into covenant with us has saved us from our sins and granted us righteousness, peace, and life through faith in his Son. He has delivered us from the power of sin, from the demonic forces which kept our minds in spiritual darkness, from the curse of the law, from the notion that we can save ourselves by obedience to the law, and from all our futile attempts at such obedience. We are the Lord's *freed* people.

Learning who we are

As Paul moves from the allegory to its application to his readers, he begins with who we are: 'Now you, brothers, like Isaac, are children of promise' (v. 28). God promised Abraham not only numerous *physical* descendants (beginning with Isaac), but also a vast *spiritual* family. That promise has been fulfilled in the multitude of believers who, like Abraham, have been justified by faith.

Learning what we may expect to face

In verse 29, Paul takes the story of the two sons and their respective mothers a stage further: 'At that time the son born in the ordinary way persecuted the son born by the power of the Spirit.' The details can be found in Genesis 21. When Isaac was being weaned (he was probably about three years old), his older brother Ishmael (who was his senior by fourteen years) mocked him. Paul declares that mocking to have been a species of persecution and says that the very same thing is happening in his own day: 'It is the same now' (v. 29).

The apostle is thinking about Christians suffering at the

hands of Jews. Just as Ishmael persecuted Isaac, so those of whom Ishmael is a picture (the Jews in their spiritual slavery) were persecuting those of whom Isaac was a picture (those who were spiritually free). History has continued to repeat itself, but on a broader scale. 'The persecution of the church, of Christian believers who trace their spiritual descent from Abraham, is not always by the world, who are strangers unrelated to us, but by our half-brothers, religious people, the nominal church.'[3] Roman Catholics, orthodox Jews, Muslims, members of the Christian orthodox communities—all claim some connection with Christ, Abraham, or both and have been chargeable with the same kind of hostility towards the children of promise that Ishmael displayed in his mocking of Isaac. It is what we are to *expect*.

Learning what we may joyfully anticipate

The declaration of Scripture that 'the slave woman's son will never share in the inheritance with the free woman's son' (v. 30) does not mean that Ishmael was denied all God's blessings. In his kind providence, God was very good to Ishmael. It would, however, only be Isaac and his offspring who would enjoy the blessings of the inheritance God had promised Abraham. That family line alone would inherit the land of Canaan and be God's special people.

For those who are Isaacs in a spiritual sense—children of promise like him—there is also an inheritance. God in his providence is certainly good to the *whole* human race. But it is only those who have faith in Christ whom he has made his heirs. God has an inheritance for believers, a first instalment of which we already enjoy in our possession of life and the

Spirit. One day, he will assuredly bring us into the fullness of this inheritance.

Learning how we are to act

Paul brings his application of the story to its climax in Galatians 5:1: 'It is for freedom that Christ has set us free. Stand firm, then, and do not let yourselves be burdened again by a yoke of slavery.' Christ has given his people freedom, and that freedom is to be jealously guarded.

There are, of course, certain respects in which we are *not* free as Christians. We are not free, for example, to live as we please. God has a rule of life for his new-covenant people as surely as he did for his people under the old covenant. In regard to the matters Paul is addressing in Galatians, however, we *are* free. From the Mosaic law as a whole, from the penalty of having broken those elements of it that are universally binding, and from all erroneous notions that we must labour to please God in order to be right with him—from all this Christ has set us free! And we are to *stand firm* in that freedom, resisting all attempts to enslave us.

FOR FURTHER STUDY

1. What are some of the other indicators in Paul's letters that the hurt inflicted by Christians whom he loved did not diminish his loving concern for them? What lessons can both pastors and Christians in general learn from his love?

2. Paul reminds the Galatians at 4:8 of the influence of demons in their pagan, unconverted days. What other pointers are there in Scripture to the influence of the demonic in false religions and their worshippers?

TO THINK ABOUT AND DISCUSS

1. In what circumstances can the affection the Galatians had for Paul at the first be kindled in the hearts of believers today?

2. Does Paul's allegorization of the mothers and sons story give us leave to do the same with other Old Testament narratives?

3. According to one writer, when Paul quotes the exhortation 'Get rid of the slave woman and her son' (v. 30), 'it was a not-too-subtle way of saying that the Galatians needed to drive the Judaizers and their legalism right out of the church'.[4] What would be the practical outworking of that in the church today?

4. Why are Christians so vulnerable that an exhortation to stand firm in our liberty is necessary?

7 On teaching that harms, and its teachers

(5:2–12)

These verses are a healthy counteractive. They illustrate how damaging is teaching that undermines the gospel of God's grace, and how important that it be opposed and its teachers with it.

Paul is anxious about the Galatians submitting to circumcision—he sternly warns them against it, in fact. Why? At a physical level, circumcision is simply a minor surgical operation, while as a religious ceremony (as Paul admits in v. 6), it is of no consequence: 'in Christ Jesus neither circumcision nor uncircumcision has any value.' Spiritually we are none the better for getting circumcised and none the worse for not. So why all the fuss?

The answer, in short, is what was being *said* about circumcision. Certain men were teaching that it was a divinely imposed obligation and that if the Galatians did not submit to it, they could not be saved. And the Galatians were believing this! Little wonder that Paul was so alarmed! This, as we have seen, was nothing less than deadly error, a perversion of the gospel of Christ (1:6–7). It was time to make a fuss!

But what does all this have to do with us? A very great deal! Circumcision, as we encounter it in Galatians, symbolizes something all too commonly encountered. It stands for every good work, every religious ceremony, and every effort after obedience that people think is necessary in order to be right with God. It stands for a religion that is all about doing one's best and trying one's hardest, a religion that is focused on working and meriting, rather than trusting wholly to Jesus. Dressed in these different clothes, the error that invaded the Galatian churches is alive and well in the world (and church) today. We need to give the apostle's words our closest attention.

You need to think about Christ! (v. 2)

Paul's opening words are very sobering: 'Mark my words! I, Paul, tell you that if you let yourselves be circumcised, Christ will be of no value to you at all' (v. 2). Who gets the benefit of Christ's Calvary work? It is the person who makes Christ the sole object of his or her trust. We must be looking *exclusively* to Jesus if the fruits of his work are to be ours. And if things should change in this respect, if we should begin to place our confidence in other things—the modern equivalents of circumcision—Christ will be of no value to us. We will gain nothing from him.

The Puritan William Perkins put it like this: '… he must be a perfect Saviour or no Saviour.'[1] With Christ, it is all or nothing. To be regular in attendance at church, to give generously to the offering, to submit to baptism, to participate in the Lord's Supper—these, for Christians, are *good* things. They are, however, useless as grounds of acceptance with God. If we would be saved from our sins, Christ must both begin and continue to be our *only* hope of salvation.

You need to think about the law! (v. 3)

The Galatians needed to understand that circumcision was part of a package. Sinai had made it an integral part of the Law of Moses. And there could be no picking and choosing. To admit that *circumcision* was binding was to admit the rest of the law to be binding as well: 'I declare to every man who lets himself be circumcised that he is obligated to obey the whole law' (v. 3).

Now, remember what was at stake. Men were telling them that circumcision was necessary for salvation. 'Well,' says Paul, 'if that is the case, you need to understand that a great deal more is required. You can't be selective. If salvation is to come through the keeping of the law, it's going to have to be through keeping the whole law and not just a part of it.' And therein lay the problem! Could they keep the whole law? Impossible! They were all law-breakers and therefore under its curse (3:10). Their one hope lay in the Jesus who had died for their redemption (3:13).

It is no different with us. If we want to travel to heaven under our own steam we must do everything right and nothing wrong. The demands of God's law must be met by us in their entirety so that at the end of life we can present ourselves to God perfect. Is that possible? We know that it isn't! There is only *one* way to God for us, and that is through Jesus.

You need to think about grace! (v. 4)

In verse 4 Paul charges those who were 'trying to be justified by law' with having been 'alienated from Christ', with having 'fallen away from grace'. The language points not to the *loss* of salvation (as is often supposed) but to an alteration in their thinking about *obtaining* salvation. Their whole stance had changed. No longer were they beggars, hands outstretched to receive salvation as a free and unmerited gift. Instead they were workers, looking for a wage. They had stepped out of the realm of *grace*. That was a tragic step to take, for salvation is by grace and grace alone (Eph. 2:5, 8). How urgently they needed to repent!

Do *you* need to repent? Like the Galatians you acknowledge the importance of believing in Jesus, but is he still your *sole* confidence? Or have you been adding certain things to the basis of your assurance? Is your hope of eternal life, at least in part, now based on the good person that you are and the good life you are endeavouring to live? If so, you have done what the Galatians did. You have stepped out of the realm of grace and need to understand how serious a matter that is. The only people who are saved (and who can rightly consider themselves to

> The only people who are saved are those who come to Christ in their helplessness and remain before him all their days in absolute dependence upon him.

be saved) are those who come to Christ in their helplessness and remain before him all their days in absolute dependence upon him. Your cry from first to last must be, 'Thou must save and *thou alone*'.[2]

It is therefore obvious that the teaching the Galatians were receiving was harming, not helping, them. In verses 7–12 the apostle had a number of pointed things to say about it.

It was keeping them from obeying the truth (v. 7)

The Christian life is compared in Scripture to a *race*. The race starts at the outset of the Christian life, ends when we enter heaven, and is to be run with perseverance (Heb. 12:1). Using this analogy, Paul compares the Galatians to athletes hindered in their race because someone has 'cut in' on them, tripping them up or elbowing them out of the way. In plain language, they were being kept from 'obeying the truth' (v. 7).

The truth in question was the truth of the gospel (compare 2:5, 14). Through the influence of the false teachers the Galatians had stopped looking wholly to Christ (as the gospel commands us to do) and were now placing their hopes in other things as well.

We may judge of the harmfulness of the teaching *we* hear by the same criteria: Does it hinder us from obeying the truth of the gospel? Does it undermine the necessity of repentance and faith? Or, as here, does it divert our gaze from Christ and fix it on other things—on our own good works, our efforts to keep the law, our connection with a certain church, or our participation in the sacraments? If so, it is harmful teaching—deadly, in fact—and we need to turn a deaf ear to it.

It was certainly not from God (v. 8)

At the beginning of his letter Paul expressed astonishment that his readers were 'so quickly deserting the one who called [them] by the grace of Christ' (1:6). They had been the recipients of a gracious divine calling. God had so blessed to them the gospel they had heard from Paul that they had come to trust in the Saviour. Would this same God now author a gospel that fundamentally contradicted the original? To ask was to answer: 'That kind of persuasion does not come from the one who calls you' (v. 8).

How do we know if someone's teaching really *is* from God? Or better, what are the marks of a 'gospel' that is *not* from God? The answer lies in its deviations from the divine original found in the apostolic literature of the New Testament—specifically in relation to grace. Does it nullify grace? Does it turn our eyes away from Jesus? If so, it does not come from the God who calls.

Its harmful effects would spread (v. 9)

Paul's warning in verse 9 that 'A little yeast works through the whole batch of dough' is also heard in 1 Corinthians 5, where the concern is with the defiling effects of an immoral man on the whole congregation. Such a man needs to be removed. Here in Galatians 5 the proverb is used in connection with harmful teaching. If the teaching isn't stopped, it will eventually damage the entire church.

False teaching, in other words, is subject to the same law that governs yeast. Its harmful effects spread. What a melancholy witness is borne to that truth throughout church history! That is why false teaching must be given no quarter. Teaching that robs us of our liberty in Christ and threatens to enslave us again is too dangerous to be tolerated. Its tendency is to spread and harm more and more people. At the earliest possible opportunity it must, if possible, be stopped.

It would be defeated! (v. 10)

When the apostle said at the beginning of verse 10, 'I am confident in the Lord that you will take no other view', he was expressing his confidence as to what the eventual outcome would be. God would bless the letter to the Galatians' recovery. By means of it they would be persuaded of the truth and delivered from their error. There might be exceptions among those who had never truly been converted in the first place, but in the church as a whole, eyes would be opened and the harmful teaching repudiated.

Lying at the back of this is the deeply comforting truth to which the same apostle gave expression in his letter to the Philippians: '... being confident of this, that he who began a good work in you will carry it on to completion until the day of Christ Jesus' (Phil. 1:6). God is committed to bringing us to heaven! In the

> God is committed to bringing us to heaven!

outworking of that he will counteract the influence of false teaching and deliver us from its damning effects.

That does not mean that false teaching is not dangerous and that the warnings of God's Word are unnecessary. In the case of his elect, however, God will ensure that the warnings are heeded and that truth and not error will triumph. It is *for* that end that letters like Galatians are in our Bibles, and *to* that end that God blesses them.

It would result in divine judgement (v. 10)

James advises that 'Not many … should presume to be teachers … because … we who teach will be judged more strictly' (James 3:1). It is a serious matter being a teacher of God's Word—especially if we teach it so falsely that those who believe what we teach will be damned. That is to be in the most perilous position imaginable! In Galatians 1 Paul pronounced terrible anathemas on such teachers (1:8–9). Here in chapter 5 he declares that 'The one who is throwing you into confusion will pay the penalty, whoever he may be' (v. 10). Such a teacher may be caring and kindly, perfectly sincere, morally upright, and passionate about what he believes, but if he is teaching deadly error, God will ultimately send him to hell.

> It is a serious matter being a teacher of God's Word—especially if we teach it so falsely that those who believe what we teach will be damned.

That being so, we ought surely to pray for such men (and women) that God, in his great mercy, will 'grant them repentance leading them to a knowledge of the truth, and that they will come to their senses and escape from the trap of the devil, who has taken them captive to do his will' (2 Tim. 2:25–26). And what a great incentive to do so when we learn from church history of God hearing just such prayers!

It certainly wasn't Paul's teaching! (v. 11)

The question with which verse 11 begins—'Brothers, if I am still preaching circumcision, why am I still being persecuted?'—suggests that rumours were abroad that Paul was now preaching the very same thing as the troublers in Galatia. What nonsense! If it *were* so, he would not be suffering persecution.

The 'offence of the cross', to which reference is made in the second half of verse 11, explains this persecution. Many of Paul's Jewish and Gentile hearers reacted very negatively to his preaching of Christ crucified. To the Gentiles, it was foolishness; to the Jews, blasphemous. How could a man who died on a cross be the promised Saviour of the world?

To those whom God has called, however, Christ crucified is 'the power of God and the wisdom of God' (1 Cor. 1:24). And that is why we continue to preach him. The cross remains a stumbling block to belief. Reactions to it are still deeply negative, but to those to whom God blesses it, it is the wisest, most powerful, most life-changing of messages.

It angered and disgusted (v. 12)

Our section concludes on a note that sounds crude to us: 'As for those agitators, I wish they would go the whole way and emasculate themselves!' (v. 12). It is helpful to note, however (and the Galatians would have been familiar with this), that self-castration was a not-uncommon pagan practice. The priests of Cybele in northern Galatia, for example, practised it in order to gain the favour of the gods. Furthermore (and Paul has made this point earlier, in Gal. 4:8–10), the false teachers' endeavour to draw the Galatians away from Christ was tantamount to drawing them back to paganism. Indeed, with their insistence on a bloody ritual, they were behaving like the *devotees* of paganism. Perhaps, then, what Paul is saying is this: 'Let them be consistent! Let them take things to their logical conclusion! If they will behave like pagan priests, let them do what pagan priests do and emasculate themselves!' That would certainly tear the mask off. It would show that the kind of religion these men were advocating was simply the old paganism in a Jewish dress, and perhaps bring some of their naïve followers to their senses.

But what does it have to say to us? This, at least: God-dishonouring, soul-imperilling, grace-negating, Christ-marginalizing, and freedom-robbing teaching of the kind being heard in Galatia ought to be regarded by us with the deepest detestation—and its teachers likewise. We must regard such teachers as servants of the devil (2 Cor. 11:13–15) and have no Christian fellowship with them. We ought not to meet with them for prayer, have joint services with them, or encourage them in their labours in any way (see 2 John vv. 7–11), but instead speak out against them as God gives us opportunity.

For further study ▶

FOR FURTHER STUDY

1. Some Christians deny that to repent of sin and believe in Christ is the sinner's *duty*. It is clear, however, from Galatians 5:7 that the gospel is something we are to *obey*. What other passages of Scripture teach the same truth?

2. At the end of 5:6 Paul says that 'The only thing that counts is faith expressing itself through love'. Where else in Paul's letters is a close connection drawn between faith and love? Why are the two so invariably found together? What are the implications of a faith that does *not* come to expression in love?

TO THINK ABOUT AND DISCUSS

1. What are the 'circumcision equivalents' (in addition to those mentioned in the exposition) that people are insisting on today?

2. What examples can you think of from church history, both of the evil effects of false teaching and of the conversion of those from whom false teaching once came?

3. What are some of the contemporary reasons why people find the preaching of the cross foolish or offensive?

4. How can we show Christian love to those who are teaching deadly error and yet at the same time express our detestation both of them and of their teaching?

8 Living as free men and women

(5:13–26)

'God has so created human nature that without the Holy Spirit it can not have any virtue or holiness.'[1] Little wonder, then, that in the Spirit's absence our lives should be full of sin! To every believer, however, the Spirit has returned, creating in us holy desires, enabling us to bear his fruit, and empowering us to resist temptation. We are incalculably in his debt.

It is striking that Paul should begin this section with a negative. He is giving instructions on Christian living to men and women whom God has called to be 'free' (v. 13), yet the first thing he does is to impose restrictions! 'But do not use your freedom to indulge the sinful nature; rather, serve one another in love' (v. 13). The freedom we have in Christ is certainly wide-ranging. We are free from Mosaic legislation (taken as a whole), free from the law's condemning power, free from having to labour to please God in order to be justified, free from the power of sin

(Rom. 6). Christians are the freest people on earth! We are not at liberty, however, to live as we please. Our freedom has bounds to it and is to be used for specified purposes.

On the one hand, we are not at liberty to sin. A more exact translation of verse 13 would substitute 'flesh' for the NIV's 'sinful nature'. 'Sinful nature', however, satisfactorily conveys the apostle's meaning. Man's nature as corrupted by sin is what is evidently upon Paul's mind. There is no escaping the implication of his words. A warning against indulging the sinful nature would be unnecessary if our sinfulness had been eradicated. Yet, however advanced in godliness we may be, our hearts are still corrupt. And we must not give in to their corrupt desires, for to do so would be to *relinquish* our freedom. It would be to put ourselves back under that cruel dominion from which the Saviour set us free (Rom. 6). The sinful nature is to be resisted, not indulged, and later in this chapter we will be reflecting on how the Spirit enables us to do that.

On the positive side, we are to 'serve one another in love', in support of which Paul goes on to say that 'The entire law is summed up in a single command: "Love your neighbour as yourself"' (v. 14). Taking it as a whole, as God's way of relating to his people and regulating their lives, the Mosaic law is no longer binding on us. Nevertheless, those elements of it that belong to the original order of things are of abiding authority. A case in point is this command concerning neighbour love (see Lev. 19:18), which sums up in one the whole of our obligation to our fellow human beings. Far from being at liberty to pander to our selfishness, we are, in obedience to this far-reaching directive, to selflessly and lovingly serve one another.

The extent of the problem (vv. 13–21, 26)

The passage leaves us in no doubt as to the kinds of things to which our sinful natures prompt us. In verse 15, for example, we have a warning against 'biting and devouring each other', a warning which, if unheeded, will result in us being 'destroyed by each other'. Again, at the end of the chapter, we are exhorted to 'not become conceited, provoking and envying each other' (v. 26). And in between there is that most disturbing list which Paul gives us in verses 19–21. A number of comments may be made on it.

It is not exhaustive. Paul ends his list with these three telling words, 'and the like' (v. 21). What he has given us is only a selection; many more sins could have been added.

It shows us what our hearts are like. What Paul is listing are the 'acts of the sinful nature' (v. 19). They originate in our sinful hearts. In Jesus's words, 'All these evils come from inside' (Mark 7:23). There may be all kinds of things that keep them in check, but beneath the outward decency the human heart is like an active volcano ready to erupt at any time.

> Beneath the outward decency the human heart is like an active volcano ready to erupt at any time.

It shows us of what even true Christians are capable. Paul's object in listing these sins was not to bring unbelievers under conviction but instead to warn his fellow Christians. It wasn't for the first time, either (v. 21).

There was not a sin on that list which they were incapable of committing, and we are in no better case. That is not to downplay the magnitude of the change in our lives if we are truly united to Christ, but it is to be realistic. Our sinful hearts continue to pose the gravest of threats to us.

It discloses what will happen if we capitulate. Paul winds up his list by saying, 'I warn you, as I did before, that those who live like this will not inherit the kingdom of God' (v. 21). They will, in other words, forfeit the fullness of the blessing that God has prepared for his people. This does not mean that if a Christian falls into one or more of these sins it is all up with him or her. Paul is not speaking here about occasional lapses—serious as these may be. He has full capitulation in mind, a surrendering to our sinful desires so unchallenged and persistent that these sins become habitual features of our lives.

It is a warning to the unholy. Do not imagine that if you are giving free rein to your sins you will still inherit the kingdom of God. Heaven is for the holy. Unless there is repentance, your unholiness will exclude you from God's blessing for ever.

> Unless there is repentance, your unholiness will exclude you from God's blessing for ever.

But it is also a warning to the holy. One of the ways in which the Lord keeps his people persevering in their warfare with sin is by making it plain to them what will happen if their warfare ceases. It is perfectly true that *real* Christians—by virtue of their union with Christ—will not give up the fight. But it is equally true that we *must not* give up, for if we do there will be no eternal blessing for us.

The answer to the problem (vv. 17–18)

As we begin to reflect on how the Holy Spirit helps us in this warfare, we note what is said in verse 17: 'For the sinful nature desires what is contrary to the Spirit, and the Spirit what is contrary to the sinful nature. They are in conflict with each other, so that you do not do what you want.' It is another of those strokes of realism for which we are so grateful in Paul's writings. He didn't paint a picture of conflict-free Christianity that no one would recognize. He was only too familiar with conflict himself. In Romans 7 we hear him crying out, 'What a wretched man I am! Who will rescue me from this body of death?' (Rom. 7:24), so intense was the struggle, so inescapable his sin, the perfection he longed for being still so far beyond him. Here in Galatians 5 he presents this same conflict as the norm for his fellow believers.

In the mercy of God, believers have experience of it in *both* its parts. We are not only familiar with the desire of our sinful natures for what is contrary to the Spirit (contrary, that is, to his wishes and his holy character), we are also familiar with the Spirit opposing our wishes with his. As a divine person, he naturally desires the opposite of all the terrible things to which our wicked hearts prompt us, and through his gracious indwelling and ministry we come to desire these opposites too. As God's agent he 'works in [us] to will' what is in accordance with God's good pleasure (Phil. 2:13).

The presence in our hearts of such diametrically opposed desires results in conflict. Don't we sometimes feel as if we are being pulled in two different directions, indwelling sin wanting one thing, the Spirit moving us to want the opposite? And if we are honest, we have to confess that the outcome is not always a good one. When Paul says at the end of 5:17 that we do not do what we want, it is likely that he is thinking about our remaining sin preventing us from always doing what in our Spirit-renewed hearts we would prefer to do—the very thing he laments in himself (Rom. 7:15–25).

Nevertheless, 'we are not under law' (Gal. 5:18). Paul means by that that we are no longer unregenerate, helpless before a law which commands us to do this and that but which offers us no assistance, condemns us for our transgressions, and extends to us no forgiveness. Instead we enjoy the leading of the Spirit (v. 18), a ministry that enables us not only to know the right way to take but also to actually take it. The outcome of the conflict, in other words, is by no means always defeat!

Walking in the Spirit (vv. 16, 25)

Thus far our focus has been on the *Spirit's* work: how in opposition to the desires of the flesh he works in us his own holy desires. There is also a very decided emphasis, however, on what *we* must do. In verse 16 we are instructed to 'live by the Spirit' (literally, to 'walk in the Spirit'), and in verse 25 to 'keep in step with the Spirit'. It is as if the Spirit gives us our marching orders and leads us forward, our own duty being to keep in step with him as he does so and go where he would take us.

The analogy must not be pressed too far—otherwise we end up with an image in our minds of the Spirit *outside* us and doing nothing more than directing us. In that case, his role would be no different from the law. But his role *is* different. Though he leads us in the path marked out for us by the commandments, he is also with us and in us to help us to take that path.

And *our* role? Since we cannot live our Christian lives independently of the Spirit, we ought never to make the attempt. We should constantly be looking to him for those things that we so much need—the knowledge of what is right and the power to choose it. He has his means—public and private—by which he communicates this light and power, and we should make the very best use we can of them.

> Since we cannot live our Christian lives independently of the Spirit, we ought never to make the attempt.

And if we do so? In the strength given to us for the path marked out for us we will live the kind of life he intends us to live. We will not 'gratify the desires of the sinful nature' (v. 16) but will instead exhibit the Spirit's fruit (vv. 22–23).

The fruit of the Spirit (vv. 22–24)

The qualities listed in these verses are said to be the *Spirit's*. They only appear in our lives because *he* is in our lives. Their presence constitutes one of the great proofs of his indwelling; their absence indicates that *he* is absent.

There are clearly many aspects to the Spirit's work. A man who wants to take an old, rusty, worn-out car and repair and restore it to such an extent that he can proudly exhibit it at a vintage car show has his work cut out for him! And when the

Spirit sets himself to repair and restore *us*, he has his work cut out for *him*. What a mess we are in by nature! What damage sin has wrought! There are just so many aspects to the job! And what an illustration we have of that in the ninefold fruit of the Spirit! We are evidently deficient in every one of these qualities since the Spirit needs to produce them in us in order to make us like Christ.

There is something distinctive about his work. In one sense, the fruit of the Spirit is common to humanity as a whole. Unbelievers can love, have joy and peace, and be patient, kind, good, faithful, gentle, and self-controlled. The whole list can be found in hearts and lives from which the Spirit is totally absent.

In what sense, then, are love, joy, peace, and so on, distinctively the fruit of the *Spirit*? The question can be answered in this way: the role of the Spirit is to take common qualities and do something special with them—something that only *he* can do by his presence and ministry in the sinner's heart. Take *love* as an example. It is present in both Christians and non-Christians alike. But it is only the Christian who loves *God* and, out of love for God, *obeys* him. It is only the Christian who loves *Christians*—loves them *because* they are Christians and out of that love endeavours to serve them. The Spirit does something unique with love. In his hands it has new objects, springs from new motives, and comes to expression in new ways.

The goal of his work is a beautiful all-roundedness. In most of us there is an unevenness about the way in which these qualities are present and come to expression. One Christian may be singularly loving and yet a prey to anxious fears. Another may be joyful and yet not very patient. A third may be exceedingly kind and yet weak in certain areas of self-control. A fourth, resolutely faithful but at times far from gentle.

In this respect we are all so different from Jesus. No one characteristic 'stood out' in him beyond the others. He wasn't strong in one area and not so strong in others; there was a beautiful all-roundedness about his life as a man of God. Each aspect of the Spirit's fruit he displayed to perfection. And it is this all-roundedness that is the Spirit's goal as he works in each of us. He will succeed in producing it, too! The same exquisite symmetry that we see in the life of the Son of God will one day be as clearly seen in *our* lives.

And in the meantime? We need to walk in the Spirit! For it is as we do so that sin is increasingly put to death and the fruit of the Spirit ripens.

For further study ▶

FOR FURTHER STUDY

1. Our passage clearly indicates that a sinful nature remains in the believer. What other evidence is there in Scripture for this?

2. The Spirit desires the opposites of those acts of the sinful nature listed in Galatians 5:19–21. What are those opposites?

3. Galatians 5:21 is not the only place where the unholy are warned that they will be excluded from the fullness of kingdom blessing. What are some of the other places?

4. In the above commentary, only one example (love) was given of what the Spirit does with the common qualities listed in verses 22–23 to make them distinctively his fruit. Go through the rest of the list, working out how the Spirit does the same with each one.

TO THINK ABOUT AND DISCUSS

1. There is a hidden paradox in Paul's language in verse 13. The word translated 'serve' means to 'serve *as slaves*'. The new life that we have, by grace, been set free to live is to be marked by loving, humble, self-sacrificial service of our fellow Christians. In what ways are we to serve one another? In what ways has Jesus exemplified such service?

2. What are the public and private means of grace that the Spirit uses to communicate knowledge and strength to us? How important is it for our warfare with sin and for living a holy life that we make use of these means?

3. What are some of the ways in which Christ exhibited the fruit of the Spirit in his own human life?

9 What does it mean in practice?

(6:1–10)

For Paul, it is never enough simply to teach doctrines and extract from them broad principles of conduct. He must always descend to practicalities, providing us with concrete examples of what living out the doctrines and principles involves. That is what we find him doing as he moves from chapter 5 into chapter 6.

Paul's burden has been that we should walk in the Spirit (5:16), that we should keep in step with the Spirit (5:25)—in other words, that we should look to the Spirit for guidance and strength and follow him as he directs us how to live. But what does that mean in practice? In the first half of chapter 6 he gives us an important part of the answer.

Restoring those who have fallen (v. 1)

He begins with the sobering reality of believers being 'caught in a sin'. What does Paul have in mind? Perhaps he is thinking of situations like that of the woman caught in adultery in John 8. They are 'found out' before any repentance has taken place. Alternatively, he may be envisaging a situation where sin takes believers 'by surprise', as it were. Their sinful acts are unpremeditated. Temptation has suddenly taken hold of them, and they have yielded. Either way, there has been sin of sufficient seriousness for them to need the restorative ministry of a fellow believer.

What an interesting word the apostle uses here! In secular Greek the word translated 'restore' was a medical term for the setting of a broken or dislocated bone. It is also used in Mark 1 of James and John mending their nets (Mark 1:19). The objects in question were 'restored' because something had gone wrong with them and they needed to be fixed. Here in Galatians 6 it is the *believer* who has gone wrong. He or she has deviated from the right path and needs to repent and return to it, and live again in the right way. And that is our goal as we address such a situation. We do not speak to such people about their sin in order to alleviate our own consciences. Our aim is their restoration to fellowship with Christ.

> We do not speak to people about their sin in order to alleviate our own consciences. Our aim is their restoration to fellowship with Christ.

Paul says that the restoring is to be done by those who are *spiritual*. By this he probably means those who are spiritually mature. Alternatively, he may be thinking of those Christians who are seeking earnestly to walk in the Spirit and bear the

Spirit's fruit. Given the difficulty and delicacy of the task, and the need for it to be handled in the right way, it is evidently such Christians who by grace are best fitted for it.

The restoring is to be done with *gentleness*. We must only attempt it in a spirit of meekness and humility. How important this is is apparent from the concluding part of the verse, where Paul instructs us to watch ourselves lest we also be tempted. Tempted to what? Perhaps to the very same sin. Or perhaps to spiritual pride. Isn't it easy to feel a little superior and self-righteous when dealing with sin into which we ourselves have not fallen? Hence the need for meekness, for humility. There is no room for harshness or pride when dealing with the fallen.

Supporting those who are burdened (v. 2)

Christians have burdens. The greatest of all, the burden of our guilt, has been taken away, but other burdens remain. Weakness because of old age, physical pain, sorrow over the loss of a loved one, depression of spirits, antagonism on account of our faith, loneliness, unemployment, a difficult pastoral problem, the ill-health of a spouse, the rebelliousness of a child, conflicts at work—such are some of the burdens (and the list could easily be extended) that in the providence of God believers may be called to bear.

We learn from verse 2, however, that it is not God's will that we should be left to bear them alone. Our fellow Christians are to do what they can to share or ease our burdens. There are all kinds of practical ways in which this may be done. Visiting when someone is sick, cooking a meal, doing some shopping, sending a note, calling on the telephone, praying, reading the Scriptures, showing hospitality, giving practical counsel—the ways in which we may carry one another's burdens are as varied as the burdens themselves.

We notice, too, that we *all* have a role to play in this. Paul is addressing everyone. This is a ministry for men and women alike, for office-bearers and for those who hold no office, for young as well as old, for new believers and mature believers, for the largely unburdened and for those whose burdens are heavy.

'In this way', writes Paul, 'you will fulfil the law of Christ.' What law? In all likelihood, the law of love: 'A new command I give you: Love one another. As I have loved you, so you must love one another' (John 13:34). We have been given a directive to *love* one another. And it is this that we fulfil when we engage in this important ministry of bearing one another's burdens.

Taking heed to ourselves (vv. 3–5)

Verses 3–5 are admittedly difficult verses, and there is a difference of opinion as to how parts of them are to be understood. They begin with a warning: 'If anyone thinks he is something when he is nothing, he deceives himself.' Paul is alerting us to the danger of the sinful pride that tempts us to look down on others and to draw comparisons between ourselves and them that are most decidedly not in their favour. The remedy? Certainly for one thing we need to remember that in and of ourselves—apart from God—we are nothing. We are all rebel sinners in whose flesh there dwells no good thing, who have nothing that has not been received as a free and undeserved gift, and who are only able to serve and glorify God because we are divinely enabled to do so.

Then in verses 4–5 there is a call to self-examination. I do not have to give account to God for what my *Christian brother or sister* has done, or what he or she *is*. It is in that sense that each one will have to bear his or her own load (v. 5). I will have to stand before God on the last day and give account to him for *my* work and *my* life. If I remember that and seek to act upon it, it will prevent an unhealthy preoccupation with what others are doing, and will keep me from the unfair comparisons that pride can so easily engender.

Still puzzled? The verses do have their difficulties! Their burden, however, is that we take heed to ourselves and guard against pride by remembering what we are, practising self-examination, and weighing seriously the fact that we will one day give account to God. That is the way to be the kind, loving, humble, serving Christians that the gospel calls us to be.

Sharing all good things with our instructors (v. 6)

Paul's exhortation in verse 6 suggests that the instructor or teacher is giving himself full-time to the work of teaching. Like the apostles in Acts 6, he is devoting himself to the ministry of the Word and to prayer. Certainly that is the ideal. If it is to be realized, however, those who are the recipients of the teaching must fulfil their God-given responsibility to ensure that their teacher is financially supported.

It was a matter on which Jesus himself spoke: 'the worker is worth his keep' (Matt. 10:10). It was only right that his disciples should be supported by the people to whom they ministered the Word. Then we have Paul's words in 1 Corinthians 9: 'If we have sown spiritual seed among you, is it too much if we reap a material harvest from you?' (1 Cor. 9:11). Or again, '... the Lord has commanded that those who preach the gospel should receive their living from the gospel' (1 Cor. 9:14).

Isn't it a fair exchange? The servant of God lays himself out for the people—labouring to bring them the Word of God for their salvation, pouring his heart and strength into his task. Surely, in return, those who benefit from his ministry should give him adequate financial support! That way he can provide for his own and his family's needs and give himself fully to the work without anxiety about material things.

Sowing and reaping (vv. 7–8)

In leaving his practical directives for a moment to take up the theme of sowing and reaping, Paul is not going off at a tangent. Sowing to please the Spirit (v. 8) is synonymous with walking in the Spirit and keeping in step with the Spirit. The apostle is simply employing another image to express the same basic concern of this entire section of his letter—that believers' lives should be shaped and directed, not by their sinful natures, but by the Spirit.

The wrong kind of sowing

To sow to please the sinful nature (more literally, to sow to the flesh) is to give the sinful nature free rein. Or, as Paul puts it in Romans 8:12, it is to live *according* to the sinful nature. God is really not in the picture. The individuals concerned are functioning as their own gods, following their own hearts, doing what is in accordance with God's law only when it suits them to do so, and ignoring it when it doesn't. It is a way of life that comes only too naturally to the unbeliever and is one to which the true believer can be tempted to return.

In warning us against such a life, the apostle begins by saying to us, 'Do not be deceived: God cannot be mocked. A man reaps what he sows' (Gal. 6:7). We must not be misled into thinking that God can be fooled in this matter. There is no escaping the fundamental law of sowing and reaping: the seed that we sow determines the

> There is no escaping the fundamental law of sowing and reaping: the seed that we sow determines the harvest that we reap.

harvest that we reap. If we sow to please the sinful nature we will 'reap destruction' (v. 8), or more exactly, 'corruption'.

This is an aspect of eternal punishment to which we perhaps do not give sufficient attention. In a way that we cannot fully understand, the sinner in hell will deteriorate, slipping ever further from what he or she was originally created to be. The ruinous effects of sin will become more and more pronounced. Endlessly, there will be movement in the wrong direction—away from God and what is good and right—and with it, an inevitable deepening of the sinner's frustration, dissatisfaction, bitterness, discontent, self-loathing, and misery.

The right kind of sowing

What is it to sow to please the Spirit? It is to cultivate the Spirit's fruit. It is to follow the Spirit's leading as he insists that we put sin to death. It is to obey him as he directs us by the commandments of Scripture. It is to resist the temptation to neglect the priceless means that he uses to enable us to grow, and instead to make the very best use of them that we can. And none of that is easy! It means daily and often painful self-denial, and may expose us to danger, bring us into conflict with unbelievers, and upset our fellow Christians.

See, however, what a harvest we will ultimately reap: 'the one who sows to please the Spirit, from the Spirit will reap eternal life' (Gal. 6:8). Eternal life is, of course, already ours. 'He who has the Son has life,' says John (1 John 5:12)—he has it *now*. We have already come to know the only true God and Jesus Christ whom he has sent (which is what eternal life is all about—John 17:3) and to enjoy the rich blessings of their friendship. Nevertheless, there is more, infinitely more, to come. And it is this 'more' that we will reap if we continue to sow to please the Spirit. He himself will bring us into the richness and fullness of the enjoyment of God that God intends should be ours.

Isn't it this that makes the prospect of eternity so attractive to Christians? We have boundless potential for spiritual growth, for the development of our faculties, for the appreciation and enjoyment of God and his works, and in glory that potential will be

> We have boundless potential for spiritual growth, for the development of our faculties, for the appreciation and enjoyment of God and his works, and in glory that potential will be realized more and more.

realized more and more. There will be nothing static about the eternal state. Rather, there will be an endless movement in the right direction with our love for God, our knowledge of his ways, and our delight in his greatness ceaselessly expanding.

Doing good (vv. 9–10)

Christians are sons of the *God* who does good and brothers and sisters of the *Saviour* who does good; like them, we, too, are to do good. It is to be one of the distinguishing characteristics of our lives. For their temporal and spiritual benefit, both our fellow human beings in general and those who belong to the family of believers are to be the objects of Christian kindness.

Don't get weary!

The exhortation begins with a plea to 'not become weary' in doing good. It is a necessary word. To keep on doing good unweariedly can be no easy task. Doing good often makes heavy demands on us, on our time, and on our energy; and when there is little opportunity to rest and no end to the caring in sight, and we are face to face with the multiplicity of other things that demand our attention, the temptation to slacken off or even abandon the good we are doing can be intense. So, too, when doing good yields poor results, when all our efforts on others' behalf seem largely, even wholly, in vain. The temptation, however, is to be resisted. Demanding as it is, discouraging as it may be, we are *not* to become weary in doing good, but are instead to press on.

A great incentive

To encourage us, the apostle assures us that 'at the proper time we will reap a harvest if we do not give up' (v. 9). It is a further play on the imagery of sowing and reaping. Doing good is like sowing. If we give ourselves to it unweariedly, we will ultimately reap a harvest.

What is the harvest? One aspect of it is *the good that is done by us*. We are assured that our labour in the Lord is not in vain (1 Cor. 15:58). We really do *good* by the good that we do—though a very long time may elapse before the fruit of it appears. There was a man by the name of Luke Short, for instance, who died sometime during the eighteenth century in the Colony of Virginia. He was converted at the age of 103 through the recollection of a sermon preached by the Puritan John Flavel eighty-five years before! There is a need for patience here!

There is also *the good that will be received by us*. This is probably what is uppermost in Paul's mind. God's people will reap a rich reward in glory for the kindness they have shown. We are told in Hebrews, for example, that 'God is not unjust; he will not forget your work and the love you have shown him as you have helped his people and continue to help them' (Heb. 6:10). Jesus himself pictures the same thing vividly in Matthew 25 in the bestowal of a kingdom on those who, in showing kindness to his people, were actually ministering to him.

As we have opportunity

Under the impulse of the incentive Paul has given us we are

to do good 'as we have opportunity' (v. 10). This may mean 'as the opportunity presents itself'. It is interesting to note, however, that the Greek word translated 'opportunity' is in the singular and may also be translated 'time' or 'season'. Taken that way, the apostle is giving us an important perspective on life as a whole. It is the time of our opportunity, our season for doing good. And in view of the promised harvest, we are to make the very best use of it that we can.

Imitating God

To whom does *God himself* do good? We may answer in the words of verse 10: 'to all people, especially to those who belong to the family of believers'. Our God is good to *all*, causing his sun to rise and the rain to fall on the righteous and the unrighteous alike (Matt. 5:45). But he is especially good to *believers*—choosing them for himself, adopting them into his family, blessing them with all spiritual blessings in Christ.

In this respect we are to be God's imitators. According to verse 10, the twofold manifestation of God's care in the world is to be reflected in the lives of his people. Like God, we are to do good to *all* people—even if they are our enemies. Especially, however, are we to do good to our fellow Christians. As members of the same body, siblings in the same holy family, their claim upon our benevolence is to be considered primary.

For further study ▶

FOR FURTHER STUDY

1. What other passages of Scripture illustrate the fundamental law that we reap what we have sown?

2. What additional light does Scripture shed on the harvest we will reap for having done good?

3. How does the concept of reward harmonize with the insistence that everything we receive from God is of grace?

TO THINK ABOUT AND DISCUSS

1. Besides the help that is given to the burdened themselves, what are some of the blessings that flow from bearing one another's burdens?

2. How is the principle of the instructed sharing all good things with his or her instructor to be applied in situations where a congregation is too small to fully support a pastor?

3. Paul says in 6:10 that we are to do good 'especially' to our fellow Christians. What does this 'especially' mean in practice, both for individual Christians and for churches?

10 A final thrust at the enemy

(6:11–18)

Here Paul is once again addressing what, on the face of it, is a dead issue. For no one, for the sake of our salvation, is seeking to compel *us* to be circumcised. Nevertheless, as we follow what the apostle is saying, we find ourselves both at the heart of Christianity (namely, the cross) and at the heart of what it means to become a Christian (which is to become a new creation).

The letter to the Galatians was, as we have seen, written in order to deliver believers from misguided and dangerous zealots, men whose gospel was 'really no gospel at all' (1:7) but instead a deadly perversion of it. Here, in this final section, the apostle makes one more appeal to them. He is so concerned that these believers wake up to their danger and have nothing more to do with falsehood that before closing his letter he returns one last time to the all-important matter that occasioned it.

He does so in his own handwriting: 'See what large letters I use as I write to you with my own hand!' (v. 11). It is likely that up to this point Paul had been dictating the letter and someone else had done the writing. Before he closed, however (and this seems to have been his custom), he took the pen into his own hand to write the concluding words. He did so in large letters. Was this because of a difficulty with his eyesight? Perhaps. More likely, it was for the sake of emphasis. Just as we may capitalize or underline words in order to express their importance, so Paul here used large letters.

The falseness of their motives (vv. 12–13)

Basically, what the apostle does in this final section is to subject the troublemakers to a twofold exposure, beginning with the falseness of their *motives*. What drove these men? Motives which, though mistaken, were nevertheless honourable? Far from it!

We notice, for one thing, that there was *something that they wanted to avoid*, namely, 'being persecuted for the cross of Christ' (v. 12). Men like Paul, who rightly put the cross of Christ at the heart of what they preached, suffered persecution. Paul himself, for example, could say that he bore on his body 'the marks of Jesus' (v. 17). The Galatians' troublers, however, were anxious to avoid such persecution, and it was precisely in order to do so that they placed such an emphasis on circumcision (v. 12). They didn't go so far as to *repudiate* the cross, but out of a desire to make their lives a little more comfortable, a little less dangerous, the cross definitely took second place to circumcision in their preaching.

We notice also that there was *something in which they wanted to glory*, namely, the Galatians' 'flesh' (v. 13). They had a 'notches on the rifle' mentality. How eager they were to boast about the number of their converts! Philip Ryken imagines them 'sending a "Mission to Galatia" newsletter back to Jerusalem. "One hundred circumcised!" the headline might read.'[1] They wanted to boast in the Galatians' flesh, to glory in their success in gaining all these Galatians to their position. And the Galatians themselves needed to know this. Whatever the appearance of things, these false teachers were acting from motives rooted in cowardice and pride.

Glorying in the cross (v. 14)

What a striking contrast the apostle Paul presents: 'May I never boast except in the cross of our Lord Jesus Christ' (v. 14). What for others was an object of loathing and disgust was for Paul a thing in which to glory. Not so much in the cross itself, of course—it was nothing but a piece of wood—but in the amazing death that took place on it and the amazing person whose death it was. The object of Paul's glorying was the crucified Jesus, the Son of God who loved him and gave himself for him (2:20). The cross of Jesus—in this sense—was what Paul trusted in, rejoiced in, revelled in, lived for. It filled his horizons, engrossed his attention, and absorbed his time and energy. It was, in an entirely healthy sense, his *obsession*.[2] And rightly so! Whether we consider the exaltedness of the sufferer, the wonder of his love, the perfection of his atonement, its worldwide scope, or the greatness of the salvation that has come to us through it, there is nothing more reasonable or right than that we should 'glory … in the cross of our Lord Jesus Christ' (KJV). It truly is the very heart of Christianity.

Paul goes on to tell us how the Saviour's cross had entirely changed his relationship to the world: 'through which the world has been crucified to me, and I to the world' (v. 14). 'World' here does not mean the created universe. Far from dealing a death-blow to our relationship to the physical world, our union with the crucified Christ actually enhances our enjoyment of it:

> Heaven above is softer blue,
> Earth around is sweeter green;
> Something lives in every hue
> Christless eyes have never seen:
> Birds with gladder songs o'erflow
> Flowers with deeper beauties shine,
> Since I know, as now I know,
> I am His, and He is mine.[3]

No one has a truer, deeper appreciation of the created order than the Christian who sees in it the Father's world and is constantly moved to worship by its magnificence and beauty.

So what, then, does Paul mean by 'the world'? He is thinking about a human society that is aligned with the evil one, is under the dominion of sin, and is thoroughly anti-God in its thinking, practices, and religion. To *that* world Paul, and every other true believer, has been 'crucified'. We no longer share its outlook, live by its principles, adopt its philosophies, love the things it loves, or take its idols for our gods. Through union with the Christ who died for us our relationship to it has entirely changed. We still *live* in it, but we are no longer *of* it. Grace has made us citizens of heaven. As a consequence, our attention is now engrossed and our lives and worship shaped by the values, religion, interests, laws, and God of that altogether different and better world.

And we are thankful! For although we feel the pull of the world and confess with shame its continuing power to attract us and to tempt us, we do not want to be of it as we were before. It is a world in rebellion against God, bearing its citizens to destruction, and we are glad that through the cross of our Redeemer we have for ever escaped its corrupting and damning influences.

The falseness of their teaching (v. 15)

A man's motives can sometimes be bad while his doctrine is good. Paul himself had an experience of that in Rome when certain men were preaching Christ 'out of selfish ambition, not sincerely, supposing that they can stir up trouble for me

> A man's motives can sometimes be bad while his doctrine is good.

while I am in chains' (Phil. 1:17). Paul certainly wasn't happy with their motives, but he could nevertheless rejoice in their message, because they were genuinely preaching Christ.

In the case of the troublemakers in Galatia, it was bad news on both counts. Not only were their motives bad, their message was bad as well. The big thing for them was circumcision. The believer in Christ needed to be circumcised! But, as Paul states with great plainness in verse 15, 'Neither circumcision nor uncircumcision means anything; what counts is a new creation.'

We have touched on this in a previous chapter, but it merits repetition. When it comes to the all-important matter of being *saved*—having our sins forgiven and getting right with the God whom we have wronged—it is of no account whether we are circumcised or not. We are none the better for having the procedure, and none the worse for not. The same thing needs to be said about all the circumcision equivalents on which people are tempted to rely today. Rituals and ceremonies, good works and efforts at obedience, identification with a particular religious body and devotion to its principles—it is not their presence in our lives that saves us, and it is not their absence that accounts for us being unsaved.

What matters, what is so all-important as to admit of no substitute, is 'a new creation'. We need, in other words, to be born again. The Spirit of God must enter us and change us on the inside, remaking us in the image of God. The great matter before each of us, therefore, is not whether we have submitted to such and such a ritual or have obeyed enough or put away enough sin in order to please God. Rather it is this: Has a saving change taken place in us? Have we become a new creation by the power of the Holy Spirit? Have we been united to Jesus Christ?

> Becoming a Christian is not a matter of fixing up our broken lives by our own careful endeavours. It is all about being united to Jesus.

In another of his letters, Paul puts it this way: 'if anyone is in Christ, he is a new creation; the old has gone, the new has come!' (2 Cor. 5:17). Becoming a Christian is not a matter of fixing up our broken lives by our own careful endeavours. It is all about being united to Jesus. We need his divine life joining itself with and flowing into our lives. We need to get connected! That's how everything becomes new. And it can only happen as we come to him in our brokenness, guilt, and helplessness, looking out of ourselves to him to be the almighty and all-sufficient Saviour that we need. The union thus formed with him will not make us perfect straightaway, but it will secure for us his righteousness, his forgiveness, and his Spirit to make us holy.

Looking back on this concluding section (indeed, on the letter as a whole), we readily see what a model Paul is for church leaders. He exemplifies his own principle that 'It is fine to be zealous, provided the purpose is good' (4:18). There are many whose zeal we cannot fault but whom we cannot admire or praise. Like the Galatians' troublers, they are zealous for no good purpose. But not Paul! How open were his eyes to the dangers threatening his converts! How intensely anxious that they should believe and practise the truth! How eager to break the hold these false teachers had over them! Here is zeal that is worthy of the most careful imitation. Let those of us who are leaders make it our prayer that the Lord would give us eyes as clear, hearts as concerned, and tongues and pens as ready as Paul's to rise to our people's defence when false teaching threatens them.

A double benediction (vv. 16–18)

The letter concludes with a double benediction. In verse 16 Paul writes, 'Peace and mercy to all who follow this rule, even to the Israel of God.' By 'all who follow this rule' he means all those who, like him, are depending on the Christ of Calvary for salvation and enjoying his recreating work. By 'the Israel of God' he means the church as a whole—the entire new-covenant community of Gentile and Jewish believers.

The apostle's second benediction adds grace to the peace and mercy already invoked: 'The grace of our Lord Jesus Christ be with your spirit, brothers' (v. 18). These three blessings were just what the believers in Galatia needed for the remainder of their Christian pilgrimage. And they are just what we—indeed, *all* believers—need as well: the peace of God that surpasses all understanding to guard our hearts and minds in Christ Jesus against all anxious care; the mercy and kindness of a pitying God to minister to us in our weakness and neither break the bruised reed nor snuff out the smouldering wick; and grace to help us in all our need.

Today, of course, we have no apostle Paul breathing such benedictions on us. But we do have the intercessory ministry of our Lord Jesus Christ, whose prayers for us secure these priceless blessings. We also have a living, loving, lasting union with Christ, by virtue of which these blessings flow into our lives. For our perseverance to the end, then, both in faith and in holiness, let there be a constant upward gaze to him for each of these blessings. And let that look be not just for ourselves, but, in imitation of large-hearted Paul, for our fellow believers likewise.

FOR FURTHER STUDY

1. Where else does Paul talk about writing at least a part of his letters with his own hand?

2. We have seen how our relationship to the world has changed through the cross (Gal. 6:14). What are some of the other relationships that the Bible explicitly identifies as having been altered by the same means? How is it through the *cross* that these relationships have changed?

TO THINK ABOUT AND DISCUSS

1. In Chapter 7 we considered why the cross so arouses people's antagonism. In what ways and in what circumstances can *we* be tempted to 'avoid being persecuted for the cross of Christ' (v. 12)? How is such temptation to be resisted?

2. What bearing ought our Calvary-changed relationship to the world have on our choice of recreational activities—the music that we listen to, for example, or the literature that we read, or the things that we watch on TV?

Endnotes

Overview

1 All dates in the timeline are from F. F. Bruce, *Paul: Apostle of the Free Spirit* (Exeter: Paternoster, 1977), p. 475.

2 William Cunningham, *Historical Theology*, vol. i (Edinburgh: Banner of Truth, 1979), p. 179.

Background and summary

1 For a good example, see Leon Morris, *Galatians: Paul's Charter of Christian Freedom* (Leicester: IVP, 1996), pp. 15–20.

Chapter 1

1 Quoted in Peter Barnes, *A Study Commentary on Galatians* (Darlington: Evangelical Press, 2006), p. 49.

2 John Eadie, *A Commentary on the Greek Text of the Epistle of Paul to the Ephesians* (Grand Rapids, MI: Baker, 1979), p. 7.

3 John Stott, *The Message of Galatians* (Leicester: IVP, 1968), p. 22.

4 James Denney, *The Death of Christ* (London: Hodder and Stoughton, 1909), pp. 110–111.

Chapter 2

1 Morris, *Galatians*, p. 52.

2 Stott, *Message of Galatians*, p. 36.

3 John Brown, *An Exposition of the Epistle to the Galatians* (Marshallton, DE: Sovereign Grace Publishers, 1970), p. 58.

4 W. F. Arndt and F. W. Gingrich, *A Greek–English Lexicon of the New Testament* (2nd edn.; Chicago: University of Chicago Press, 1979), p. 891.

5 Stott, *Message of Galatians*, p. 41.

Chapter 3

1 Quoted in Stott, *Message of Galatians*, pp. 59–60.

2 Ibid., p. 55.

Chapter 4

2 R. A. Cole, *The Epistle of Paul to*

the Galatians (London: Tyndale
Press, 1965), p. 86.

Chapter 6

1 Philip Graham Ryken, *Galatians*
(Phillipsburg, NJ: P&R, 2005),
p. 172.
2 Ibid., p. 184.
3 Stott, *Message of Galatians*,
p. 127.
4 Ryken, *Galatians*, p. 191.

Chapter 7

1 Ibid., p. 199.
2 Augustus Toplady, 'Rock of
Ages'.

Chapter 8

1 Abraham Kuyper, *The Work of
the Holy Spirit* (New York: Funk
and Wagnalls, 1900), p. 102.

Chapter 10

1 Ryken, *Galatians*, p. 272.
2 John Stott, *The Cross of Christ*
(Leicester: IVP, 1986), p. 349.
3 Edward Robinson, 'Loved with
Everlasting Love'.

Additional resources

Expositions of Galatians

Peter Barnes, *A Study Commentary on Galatians* (Darlington: Evangelical Press, 2006)

John Brown, *An Exposition of the Epistle to the Galatians* (Marshallton, DE: Sovereign Grace Publishers, 1970)

Leon Morris, *Galatians: Paul's Charter of Christian Freedom* (Leicester: IVP, 1996)

Philip Graham Ryken, *Galatians* (Phillipsburg, NJ: P&R, 2005)

John Stott, *The Message of Galatians* (Leicester: IVP, 1968)

The doctrine of justification and the New Perspectives on Paul

James Buchanan, *The Doctrine of Justification* (Edinburgh: Banner of Truth, 1984)

John Murray, *Redemption Accomplished and Applied* (Part 2, Ch. 5) (Edinburgh: Banner of Truth, 1979)

Philip H. Eveson, *The Great Exchange: Justification by Faith Alone—In the Light of Recent Thought* (Leominster: Day One, 2008)

John Piper, *The Future of Justification* (Wheaton, IL: Crossway, 2007)

Cornelius P. Venema, *Getting the Gospel Right* (Edinburgh: Banner of Truth, 2006)

Guy Prentiss Waters, *Justification and the New Perspectives on Paul* (Phillipsburg, NJ: P&R, 2004)